Prai

I thank God for the courage I see unfolded in this book, a courage that gripped Sherri Cullison to the extent that she wrote such a story out of personal experience. We often read how-to books of instruction about handling various life situations that give mindful help, but Sherri's book, *SOS: A Mother's Story of Survival, Rescue, and Hope in the Darkness of Teen Suicide*, extends a hand of personal heartache of deepest emotion to bring about a resurrection of inner hope through God's help to the reader. Sherri weaves into her story of personal tragedy an element of brutal honesty that shines with heavenly brilliance, open to all who reach for rescue and victory that the Lord so willingly gives to those who sincerely seek Him. "Ask and it will be given to you; seek and you shall find ..." (Matthew 7:7 NIV).

—Denny Colvig, Hospice Chaplain

For forty years in ministry, pastoring those who have lost a loved one has been one of my duties and also one of my privileges. The death of a child or young person is particularly poignant and heartrending since we generally expect our children and young people to carry on the next generation. Only those who have experienced such a loss can fully understand the deep and devastating feeling it brings, particularly when death is by someone's own hand. I had the privilege of meeting Ray and Sherri and hearing this moving story a few years ago at an evangelistic mission in Northern Ireland, where I ministered. In this book Sherri shares the loss she and Ray and their family experienced, the dark valley they had to walk through. There is honesty here, unfathomable pain, and a lingering sense of loss. John's gospel tells us that at the tomb of his friend Lazarus, "Jesus wept" (John 11:35 NIV). Those two simple words, in the original language, mean to convey a heart-wrenching anguish that is almost inexpressible. The anguish Sherri and Ray felt is recounted in this book as well. But there is hope here too, founded on the glorious Easter fact of the resurrection and faith in the One who conquered death. Out of the apparent injustice and tragedy of Good Friday and the Cross came the triumph of Easter. Out of Sarah's story comes the strength and hope of faith that can weather the storm because it is anchored to the Rock that is Jesus Christ. Listen to this story as Sherri opens her heart and shares her faith, and be encouraged that as Corrie ten Boom, the Dutch lady imprisoned by the Nazis in World War II, once said, "There is no pit so deep that He is not deeper still."[1]

—Rev. Maurice Laverty, BD, MA (retired), Former Superintendent Minister of High Street Methodist Church, Lurgan, Northern Ireland

---

1 Corrie ten Boom with John and Elizabeth Sherrill, *The Hiding Place* (Uhrichsville, Ohio: Barbour and Company, Inc., 1971), 199.

In the day and age in which we live, more and more people struggle with the grief and sorrow of someone who has been tragically taken from them. Sherri's own experience and journey in coming to terms with her loss speaks to the power of God and His wonderful compassion and comfort. She shares with us an honest look at both the raw emotion and gracious strength that comes from trusting Jesus in these incredibly difficult times. I highly recommend this book for those who are living with this dark reality as well as those who know someone who is suffering. I am confident these words will help in the journey ahead.

—John Pool, Senior Pastor, New Life Church, Kingman, Arizona

Amidst our deepest despair, there is still hope. This is the powerful life message Sherri Cullison shares that is sure to reach down deep into the hearts of those who hurt, grieve, or cry out for comfort and peace. Surviving a terrible personal crisis—the sudden death of her beloved daughter—Sherri discovered hope in the One who not only rescued her, but also promises life-saving deliverance to all who trust Him. Life's messes are only temporary, she says, because God's purposes in our pain are beautiful—for our growth and His glory.

—Dawn Wilson, founder of Heart Choices Today and
Upgrade with Dawn, and Blogger for *Revive Our Hearts*

Too many times, during my twenty-nine years in law enforcement, I have seen the devastating effect that suicide has on families and the community. *SOS: A Mother's Story of Survival, Rescue, and Hope in the Darkness of Teen Suicide* does not attempt to make sense of the pain and tragedy of suicide, but it does testify to the indescribable peace and faithfulness of God that passes all understanding during unimaginable times. I appreciate the author's willingness to share her family's experience for the glory of the Lord and to be a help to others.

—Rusty Cooper, Chief of Police, Kingman, Arizona

Sherri and her husband, Ray, have passed through turbulent waters, seeing, hearing, and feeling the presence of our omnipotent God, rescuing them time and time again. They now help others through tough times, as this heartfelt book so wonderfully illustrates.

—George Carey, Senior Pastor, Kingman Presbyterian Church

SOS

SOS

*A Mother's Story of Survival, Rescue,
and Hope in the Darkness of Teen Suicide*

Sherri J. Cullison

Published by Redemption Press, PO Box 427, Enumclaw, WA 98022.
Toll-Free (844) 2REDEEM (273-3336)

Redemption Press is honored to present this title in partnership with the author. The views expressed or implied in this work are those of the author. Redemption Press provides our imprint seal representing design excellence, creative content, and high-quality production.

The author has tried to recreate events, locales, and conversations from memories of them. In order to maintain their anonymity, in some instances the names of individuals, some identifying characteristics, and some details may have been changed.

ISBN 13: 978-1-64645-337-5 (Paperback)
978-1-64645-335-1 (ePub)
978-1-64645-336-8 (Mobi)

Library of Congress Catalog Card Number: 2021910653

I dedicate this book to my husband, Ray, my elite encourager and biggest fan. Our daily journey isn't always easy, but I'm thankful we're in this together always and forever. Your hands, your embrace, and your heart, I hold so, so close to mine.

To my children, Raymond and Namantha. Thank you for allowing me to share our heartbreak to save lives and bring hope to others. I love you always and just as much.

Finally, to Sarah Renee. One day I'll hold you close, my baby girl. But for now, because of the cross, I know you're safe in Jesus's arms. And so am I.

Acknowledgments

To my Way Maker, my God. Without You I would be nothing. Without Your friendship and free grace, I would feel lost and incomplete. You bless me with courage and worth. You deserve every note of glory that comes my way; therefore, I lift my singing voice to the heavens to thank You because You are my greatest audience. Though we've only just begun this new endeavor, it's You and me, God, all the way.

Jo and Don Stetson. We have seen the evidence that God brought us together for a reason, a big reason. There is not one minute possibility that I could have completed this book project if it weren't for you. Therefore, you were a significant duet that was placed in the front row, if you will. Because of your obedience and trust, I am able to bring all the parts into play to create a beautiful voice of love that will rise to heaven for others. Thank you from the depth of my soul, the one that longs for hope for the world. I'm forever grateful.

My indebtedness to my team of prayer partners, appropriately entitled "Partnering for His Purpose," is equivalent to a cantata of thank-yous. The many prayers you heralded to the throne of God for me is incomprehensible. From the bottom of my heart, halfway up, and all the way to the top, I thank each and every one of you. Prayer is not just one key on the keyboard of life, but it is the whole gamut of music for the one in the center circle. It's because of your prayers that my family and I were protected and graced.

Jay Lowder. It was twenty years ago that Ray and I met you and many miles have distanced us since then, but nothing has separated us. Your willingness to share Sarah's story has led to lives being encouraged, changed, and saved. Thank you for being a profound voice in the desert for God's purposes in our lives and the lives of others. The Lord of heaven has orchestrated the parts to bring Sarah's story to the pages in hand. And you, my friend, are an invaluable soloist, a powerful voice that brings the melody of God's love.

To my many endorsers. Each of you has had an impact on my life, and I thank you. Your words of endorsement rise as a pleasant crescendo and accentuates your kindness. Your compliments are poetic and strengthen my song. May God bless you for your faithfulness as you serve Him today and forever.

To Christian Joseph. Your talent, your personality, and your understanding of music goes far beyond my comprehension. You are a true artist. By writing Sarah's song, you burst open the floodgates of healing and the compassionate door of literally hundreds of hearts. I meet people still today who tell me how that song has impacted their lives. Thank you for letting God use you to touch so many. God bless you, brother. You rock.

To my Redemption Press team. You have orchestrated a throng of amazing artists who undoubtedly know how to make music with words. With the input of each instrumental person, you have created a symphony from the simple scribbled paper cast across the floor of the studio. May God continue to sing over you.

In my distress I prayed to the Lord,
and the Lord answered me and rescued me.
Psalm 118:5 (NLT)

Contents

Foreword

by Jay Lowder

I WAS IN ARIZONA FOR A SPEAKING ENGAGEMENT WHEN I first met Sherri. I had received a phone call at my hotel from her husband asking if I could meet the two of them for lunch. I had never met either one of them. After agreeing to the meeting, I inquired from her husband the nature of the proposed visit. His answer was impossibly vague, but it was apparent that something was painfully wrong.

As I sat talking to her husband, Ray, in walked Sherri. I could tell she had been crying on the way to the restaurant. After brief introductions, she reached into her purse and did something that has been forever etched into my memory. Without any explanation, she pulled out a clear plastic sandwich bag, slid it across the table, and motioned for me to open it. Enclosed was a picture of a beautiful chocolate-haired teenage girl dressed in a cheerleader uniform. By the resemblance I could tell it was her daughter. After perusing a couple of photographs, I noticed a folded sheet of paper and began reading. It was her daughter Sarah's suicide note.

Sherri and Ray then unwrapped the agonizing story of their daughter's suicide.

In that meeting it became undeniably clear that Sherri wanted to somehow use her daughter's tragic death as a deterrent for others considering the same escape. As a result of them being aware of my own suicide attempt years earlier and my work with students worldwide, they selflessly permitted me to share Sarah's story. Since then, through Sarah's life and untimely death, tens of thousands of hurting people have discovered hope, purpose, healing, and the reasons to live. Undoubtably, Sherri's response to her daughter's death has saved countless lives and continues to be a lighthouse to many suffocating in darkness.

I was so moved by their courage and passion to rescue and aid others, I invited them to the United Kingdom to share their story in one of our events. They were phenomenal! They are true friends who inspire me to continue our work.

Few tragedies wound deeper than the suicide of a child, often leaving the survivors with the collateral damage of guilt, devastation, and the inability to answer the never-ending question of "Why?" Sherri has not only navigated these excruciating ditches, but she has also become a valuable resource and lifeline for anyone trying to cope with the suicide of a loved one. This book is more than the tragic story of losing her beautiful daughter; it is a tool for others to help them recover, heal, and make sense of the unthinkable. I have the utmost respect for Sherri and her unwavering trust in God, even when it didn't seem to make sense to do so. She is not only an incredible writer, but she is also a living testimony of a mother's love, endurance, and faith. This gripping and insightful book will not only arrest your heart, but it will become a tool to aid you or others you know who are trying to deal with loss, pain, and inconceivable suffering.

Introduction

LIFE ISN'T EASY. IN FACT, IT'S HARD. SOMETIMES IT'S REAL hard. There may be struggles in our lives that we wrestle with every day. Other times there may be things that happen that send our comfortable world spinning into chaos. Regardless of how sudden and unexpected an event is, it can disrupt and even devastate our lives.

My life has been marred by a devastating loss. My youngest daughter Sarah ultimately made the choice that life was too hard, and at fourteen years old, she tragically took her own life. No warning, no caution flag, no billboard sign—nothing to prepare me that this was coming. It was an instant moment of total shock that crashed my world.

My life became like a fragile ship thrust across angry waves in a dark, wild storm. The unprecedented trauma, depression, anxiety, and loneliness that I experienced was the most frightening display of coming face to face with darkness that I had ever experienced. I needed help to survive this tragedy. I couldn't do it alone.

Through an SOS call, hope came for me. It was my first step of recovery, even though I was still in the dark hallway of confusion. I knew I needed hope to survive. Hope meant that I had a desire for something to come—something good, something lasting. Something I could hold on to for dear life every day.

There are so many things we can enjoy that momentarily make us happy, but there is no comparison to the satisfaction we gain from the hope that comes through faith. Hurts may come, and then life will get better. And then unexpectedly, hurts may come again. Honestly, it can become a vicious circle. But believe me, God wants us to have an abundant life. He already knows it's not a bowl of cherries. He doesn't expect us to do all the work and tirelessly try to make lemonade out of lemons. God wants us to find satisfaction in each day, to have fun, and to enjoy family and friends.

Faith isn't an enormous wall we have to climb or a fight we have to win. Some days our faith may be stronger than other days, but I believe we can overcome. I'm convinced we all simply lack the belief that we can. Even though we may struggle sometimes with a lack of faith, we just need to believe we can press on with God's help.

I'm sharing my rescue story because I want you to know that God's intention isn't for us to be miserable every day. I have experienced a tremendous loss, but I also have joy because of the love He has for me no matter where I've been or what I've done.

I hope that when you read this book you'll learn that when life gets hard, you're not alone. This book will encourage you that when you're afraid and feel all alone in your heartbreak, you can have faith that God is right there with you to help you weather the storm.

I pray that the words on the pages of this book will come alive for you and speak life into your heart and give you hope. I believed long ago that I lost my life when I lost Sarah. Instead, when I realized that I can still love my life, I gained my life. Grasp hope, my dear friend, and allow yourself the freedom to love your life.

CHAPTER 1

The Ring

December 1990

The day you saved me was the day I cared
I'll always worship you, I'm always there.
—*Sarah Cullison*

MY THREE YOUNG CHILDREN, WIDE EYED WITH AWE AND wonder, crowded in front of our living room window, watching as snow fell heavily to the ground. It was collecting on the ground quickly, and so did their excitement.

"Can we go play in the snow, Mom?" Raymond, my ten-year-old son, asked, his big blue eyes wide with anticipation.

"Yeah, Mom, can we go outside and play in it?" my eight-year-old-daughter Namantha echoed, her green eyes dancing, pleading.

"Yes, but be sure to dress warm and don't forget to—" Before I finished my sentence, they screamed with delight and ran off.

"Put on your gloves and beanies," I responded to the single audience who was still there.

Sarah, my five-year-old and youngest child, now reigning over the entire window, blew her warm breath onto the glass. She doodled a picture in the cloud with her little finger, not realizing she had been left behind.

"You'd better run and get dressed so you can go play outside in the snow," I told her.

"Oh yeah," she responded, giggling.

The two oldest had run to their bedrooms to dress for their snow day. Sarah quickly trotted her way down the hallway, trying to catch up, her short brown hair bouncing with every step.

I could hear their little voices chatting with anticipation as they hurriedly dressed.

"Sarah, here, let me zip up your coat," Namantha said.

"Are you guys ready yet?" Raymond beamed as he stood at the girls' bedroom doorway. He pulled his knit cap over his head, his blond hair slipping out from underneath.

"Almost," Namantha said with a struggle in her voice. "Here, Raymond, help me zip Sarah's coat up."

"Got it," I could hear Raymond say. "Where's her hat?"

With all three dressed in coats, gloves, and hats, they stepped outside into the snow. Their smiles and fun chatter made me smile. The snow crunched as they made their way to the side yard that was wide open for play. We all played the morning away together, making snowballs and building a snowman.

Later that afternoon, my husband, Ray, came home from work, and our neighbor hooked a rope from the bumper of our pickup to an inner tube. Raymond and Namantha hopped onto the inner tube, and I put Sarah in the cab of the pickup with me. Then Ray slowly drove down the street, pulling the kids about thirty feet behind us. The windows inside the pickup fogged up, so Ray slid open the back window. Sarah spun around on her knees to look out. Other neighborhood kids stood out on the street, cheering on our fun as the neighbor's dog barked and ran alongside the pickup. I think he wanted in on the fun.

Raymond and Namantha held tight to the inner tube each time they hit a bump and slightly bounced up in the air. I could hear their chuckles along with the chatter of encouragement from the roadside cheering crowd. The snow spit itself up periodically into their faces and into their laps as Ray slowly pulled them down the street. Then it happened.

The neighbor's dog, brownish and of medium build, had kept chasing us until he decided to run to the other side of the street in between the pickup and the inner tube. The rope caught him and flipped him right into the laps of Raymond and Namantha. For a second he was in shock. He looked around as if to say, "What just happened?" Raymond and Namantha laughed, and so did the neighbor children who watched this scene of the comedic snow day. The dog quickly jumped off and thankfully was okay.

Sarah, who was inside the cab with us, watched the whole scene out the back window and saw the dog plop into their laps. She laughed and laughed and kept laughing for what seemed like hours.

Ray and I laughed at the dog, and we laughed because Sarah was so tickled at this whole scene. Every time later in the day that she thought about it, she started laughing again. It was a fun snow day, but the dog's surprised face was the icing on the cake. It was a great early Christmas present for all of us.

Christmastime was my favorite time of the year. Our home was colorfully decorated for the season. My sister-in-law Cynthia arranged to have a huge box wrapped in Christmas paper delivered to our house a few days before Christmas, a gift just for me. My husband, Ray, our three small children, Cynthia, and I gathered around the box for the unveiling.

I tried to guess what was in it, but I had no idea. "Is it a washing machine?"

I tried again. "A dishwasher maybe?" No response.

"Is it a desk or a chair?" I asked.

The box was big enough to hold every one of my guesses. Well, I was way off course.

We all stood around the wrapped box with the kids even trying to guess what was in it, each of them chattering to each other with eyes wide with excitement. I think they were just as happy to watch this as I was to open it. We even had someone take a photograph of us and the box.

I removed the big red bow on top of the box and found a spot to start ripping the wrapping paper. It wasn't long before the kids joined in. Paper tearing and more guesses filled the air. What could it be? I lifted the lid of the large box. Inside was another wrapped box. We all laughed. Inside that box was another box and so on. After five boxes were unwrapped, I held in my hand a small box that could have housed a key. It was obvious to us all it was a piece of jewelry. The excitement of unwrapping all the boxes was my sister-in-law's way of giving the gift without revealing its contents.

The chatter quieted. Everyone was quiet now with anticipation. I slowly opened the small, hinged box, and there was my mother's ring. It was beautiful. It brought tears to my eyes, not only because of its beauty but of the beauty it represented. Each of my children's birthstones were displayed in a line with the unique design of the gold ring. I loved it. I absolutely loved it. It couldn't have been more perfect. I couldn't have asked for a better gift that meant so much.

Soon winter turned into spring and with it came warmer temperatures. This was a time of new beginnings and beauty reappearing after several months of lying dormant. The trees were waving their newly sprouted, green leaves in the light breeze. My three young children were outside playing, and I decided to join them and enjoy some fresh air. The sunshine on my face gifted me with warmth and brought a smile to my face on this beautiful spring day.

The yard needed attention. New weeds were coming up, and I thought I would take advantage of the warm weather and beauty of the outdoors to do some yardwork. For some reason, our rose planter on the side of the house had collected a few inornate objects that needed to be cleaned up. Although our home had a lot of space, the yard in the front of the house was small. A chain-link fence surrounded the front of what consisted only of a line of cottonwood trees and a small sidewalk beside the stairs leading to the front door.

This day we had lived in the house for about five years. My son, Raymond, was ten years old, and my daughter Namantha was eight. My youngest, Sarah, was five. I enjoyed their giggles as they played. I began cleaning up the yard on the side of the house. The side yard was a full lot with only a fruit tree and dirt. In the Arizona springtime, weeds grew like wildflowers.

As I cleaned out the flower planter, I turned around and looked at the front yard. I thought, *Oh, how I wished we had grass and pretty flowers in this little area.* The line of trees gave some shade but not enough greenery for my delight. It was dirt and dry and dusty. Even the small cement sidewalk leading to the front door had been poured crooked. I sighed to myself and went back to work.

A couple of hours later I went in to clean up and cook dinner. As I rinsed the soap off my hands under the faucet, I noticed something wrong with my mother's ring.

The ruby stone that represented Sarah's birthstone was gone. I felt sick to my stomach, and my whole upper body dropped. Tears filled my eyes. I went back outside and looked around on the ground, but nothing. It was gone. I was so disappointed that I didn't want to cook dinner. The ring looked so empty, even though Raymond and Namantha's birthstones were still there. *My husband and his younger sister would be so upset*, I thought.

Immediately I assumed that since I had lost one stone, I could very well lose another one, so I put the ring in my jewelry box for now. My finger felt out of sorts, since I had worn the ring every day. It was one of the most meaningful gifts I had ever received.

When I first discovered Sarah's stone was gone, I was so disappointed. The heaviness of the loss of her stone brought me down emotionally. Possibly God was preparing me for something, but I didn't recognize that at that time. I felt this cloud overcome and overwhelm me even though it was the middle of spring and new life was budding everywhere.

And just as hard as it was losing the stone, I felt the sting when I had to put the ring back in my jewelry box, not knowing when I would be able to wear it again. The stone was gone—her stone—and I didn't feel it would ever be the same without it. It weighed heavy on me.

Let me ask you, what does heaviness mean to you? How does it make you feel? These days working out at the gym has become popular in our culture. When lifting those weights, it's hard. It affects your arms, your back, your knees, and other parts of your body, even your lungs. Years ago, when I went to the gym, I enjoyed lifting weights. Well, certain ones anyway.

When I sat on one particular machine, I remember sliding my shins underneath a padded iron bar that hung down. I had to lift the padded bar until my legs were nearly straight out in front of me. Attached to the bar were weights. Lifting the bar wasn't the hard part. Lowering the bar back down had to be done very slowly so that the weights didn't lower onto the stationary weights and hit hard enough to break them.

After doing ten of those leg lifts, I was overheated. Sweat rolled down the back of my neck. My stomach muscles and leg muscles ached. I didn't have anything to hold onto with my hands, so I felt like I wasn't anchored at all. Most of the pressure ended up affecting my legs the most. I was breathing heavy and about to give way and quit when this little voice in my head urged me to do two more. I felt like I was literally going to die, but I pushed myself. After the last two leg lifts, I tried getting off the lousy machine with my weak and wobbly legs. A lot of heavy amounts on weak muscles can make my body reject this tortuous behavior and make my mind want to resign from this crazy idea that doing this could make me look and feel better.

Circumstances we face in life, some rare and some every day, can put a weighted download on us mentally and even spiritually, just like the pounds of pressure at the gym. It might be as a result of not getting that job you wanted or maybe your child ends up at the emergency room, running a high fever. Maybe your husband had a hard day at work, you didn't cook dinner just like he wanted, and harsh words were said. So many things that come our way can bear weight on us— sometimes without warning.

Heaviness can develop in so many different ways, possibly as a result of harsh words from another person or even unforgiveness. Worry, fear, and doubt are all emotions that can cause heaviness to our minds and even our faith. Holding on to all of these emotions are all bad habits that can invade the faith in our minds and overtake us like a vine running rampant up a wall of an old castle. Eventually the vine can cut off any other living greenery and cause it to die. Up close it looks like a pretty plant that decorates the stone wall. From a distance it seems to overtake the wall and growl for more domination. If we choose to allow it, these troubles in our mind can overtake and overwhelm us into submitting to its domination and our spiritual health.

In the Bible in Isaiah 61:3 (NKJV), it is written that the prophecy of the coming Messiah will accomplish many things, but in verse three, it is said that He (Jesus) was sent to give us the garment of praise for the spirit of heaviness.

Yes, you can pray for whatever mess you seem to be in now, but remember those miracles He gave you before. Let your mind search and find in your memory bank that day He saved you from a car accident. And that day you thought you were being fired, but you received a raise. And of course, that time you felt no one loved you, but He showed you He did. Remember this promise in His Word.

> He is your praise; he is your God, who has done for you these great and awesome things that your own eyes have seen. (Deuteronomy 10:21 NRSV)

Think on the wonderful things you yourself have seen God do in your life and in others' lives.

Then . . .

Praise Him. Among other things, Jesus came so that He can give us the garment of praise for the spirit of heaviness. That's a God promise in Isaiah 61. Among the list of wonderful things He said He would give us, the Lord promised He will give us the garment of praise. He didn't indicate He would give it to us if we asked. It simply says He will give it to us. We need to praise Him for His holiness, His way making, and His miracles. We need to lift Him up and honor Him with our praise. Wear that garment not just for the moment but for the entire trial we face. Speak your praise and sing it to Him, and exalt the One who saved you, who rescued you, and so many other things for you before. But now, now is the time to reach up to heaven and lift your burden through praise. I promise you, my friend, that as you lift your praise, He will lift your spirit of heaviness. Remember this verse when you feel the heavy weight of circumstances in your life, for it will be in these moments that He will restore you.

Thankfully, a few years later when Namantha was a grown woman, she gave me a very special Christmas gift. As I opened the small box, there was my mother's ring with Sarah's stone replaced. What another wonderful gift. What an indescribable and thoughtful gift she gave, so unselfish, so giving. It meant everything to me. My ring is a representation of my children, my little loves, the ones I hold close to my heart. My ring had been restored with Namantha and God's help.

Praise the Lord; praise God our savior! For each day he carries us in his arms. (Psalm 68:19 NLT)

Prayer of Praise

Father, I know that troubles weigh me down, but I also know You lift me up. I praise You because You are my Counselor and my Helper. I lay all of my cares at Your feet and I surrender them to You. In my praise, I will rest in Your promise that You're with me and that You will restore what has been lost. In the worthy name of Jesus I pray. Amen.

CHAPTER 2

The Note

July 1999

Though heaven didn't need another angel
We know it's probably brighter cuz she's there.
—*Christian Joseph*

THE SUMMER OF SARAH'S FOURTEENTH YEAR WAS BUSY with special trips for her activities. Sarah always looked up to her sister Namantha who had been on the pom dance team in school. Sarah wanted to try out as well, so at the end of the previous school year, she had pom tryouts where she learned new dances and performed before judges. She had made the team for next year, her freshmen year in high school. She was so excited that her smile appeared permanent. Her hard work and persistence had paid off.

Sarah also attended youth group at our church most Wednesday nights, and we had the opportunity to go to youth camp in New Mexico. I had felt the prompting of God to go as a counselor. It was a week full of lively worship, bold teaching of the Bible, small group meaningful discussions, and time with friends. From this mother's point of view, it was also a special time with my daughter. We spent quality time together, and I allowed her quality time with her friends and new friends she made from other groups. I will treasure memories from this week for the rest of my life because it was the one time she and I had this special time together as mother and daughter, learning and experiencing God's grace and love.

One of the afternoons we had free, I went to look around in the camp gift shop. I stood there alone for probably twenty minutes trying to decide what to buy. There were T-shirts, necklaces, bumper stickers, and all the usual Christian trinkets. I stood, staring at two refrigerator magnets, and tried to decide which one to buy. I can't explain why it was so hard. Maybe because I wanted to buy the second one, but I was being tugged to buy the first one. I wrestled with deciding, maybe because I wanted what I wanted, and God was trying to tell me I should buy the first one. Finally, I gave in. I bought the first one. It's a smaller heart connected to a larger heart that says,

"I am with you always." (Matthew 28:20 NIV)

Less than two months later, on Tuesday, September 7, 1999, everything indicated Sarah was starting a new life. Summer was over and school had begun. New notebooks, new clothes, new haircut, new school, new schedule. It didn't start off well, however.

When I drove her to school that next day, I spilled my cup of hot tea onto her lap, and it was a mess. Besides the fact that it was hot, it stained her pants, and she began to cry. I apologized over and over, but her tears still flowed down her cheeks and washed away her makeup. I felt my insides crumble. I felt so badly because she was starting all these new things in her life, and on top of all of that, I let this happen.

I suggested we wipe up the mess and allow her to compose herself before going into school, but she wouldn't. She rushed out of the car to a small group of girls obviously expressing their concern why she was crying. I felt horrible about the incident the rest of the day. I felt responsible for her misery. As the day wore on, I concluded I did what I could and apologized for making a mess of things. It was up to her with how she responded and how she allowed it to affect the rest of her day.

The rest of the week was normal. Our lives went on. Sarah forgot about the tea accident. At least it appeared that way. The rest of the week we carried on as usual as we sank into the new schedules of the girls being back in school, Namantha starting her senior year and Sarah in her freshman year.

My husband, Ray, went to work early that morning, and I got my two girls off to school. My son Raymond, the older of my children, had graduated from high school the year before and was working at his job. In 1999, schools still carried on a five-day week, so I drove Sarah to school as usual on Friday, September 10, 1999.

Around three o'clock, the doorbell on my office door buzzed, notifying me that someone was at the door and needed into my office. Because I was the judicial assistant to a Superior Court judge, our office was behind secured metal doors with a security system. It was normal to let in attorneys, judges, clerks, and others through my door to carry on business. This time I saw a more familiar face in the camera above the door. It was Sarah. I was shocked, to say the least. She normally rode the bus home after school. My mind raced with horrid possibilities. I wondered *how* she had gotten from the high school to the courthouse, which are about a mile apart. I felt my heart rate increase and worry settle into my mind. I quickly buzzed her through the door to my office.

"Hi, what are you doing here? Why didn't you ride the bus home?" I asked anxiously.

"Well, I missed the bus, so I thought the best thing to do would be to come here and ride home with you," she explained with a half grin.

"How'd you miss the bus? You never miss the bus. How did you get here?" I asked inquisitively because it scared me thinking she might have gotten a ride from some stranger.

"My friend's mom gave me a ride," she said calmly.

My heart rate started to slow down. I had worried something was very wrong. I sat her down at the spare desk in my office to do some reading and homework while I worked.

"Can I type on the typewriter, Mom?" she asked with a smile.

"Yes, of course," I answered.

All of my kids enjoyed using the typewriter when they were with me in my office. The decision that I allowed her to use the typewriter is one I'm glad I made. She took a piece of plain paper and began typing. There were at least two times I remember jokingly peeking over her shoulder asking her what she was writing, but she quickly covered the paper with her arm and, while gently smiling, said it was just a note to a friend.

Later as we were getting ready to leave the office and head home, Sarah asked,

"Can we drop this letter in the mail at the post office on the way home?"

"Can it wait for another day?" I asked impatiently.

"Can we please?" she pleaded.

I was anxious to get home, but I drove through the drop off station at the post office and put the letter in the box. It was a little odd, yes, but I didn't think much of it really.

It was her last writings, her feelings written on paper to a boy she loved. And probably the last time she picked up a pen, typed on a typewriter, licked an envelope, spent time with me in my office, rode in my car, walked into our home, drank water.

I would find out later that the envelope I had dropped into the mailbox that day was my young daughter's suicide note.

I drove home that afternoon with Sarah and we talked about school, the homework she had finished, and about plans for the weekend. She was going to spend that night with a friend, and we needed to connect with the friend and her mom later on. She talked freely. Sarah didn't show any signs of anything unusual.

We got home, picked up Ray, and went to find the house where she and her friend were going to spend the night. We drove around for nearly an hour, trying to find her friend to no avail. Ray and I were driving to a movie about thirty minutes away and wanted her to come along, but she insisted on staying home.

She was fourteen years old and had stayed at home alone a few times before during short periods. We told her to call her older sister at her pizza restaurant job if there were any problems. She also had a friend a few houses down the street in case of an emergency. She knew to lock the door behind us. She knew not to cook on the stove. She knew there were leftovers in the refrigerator she could warm up in the microwave for dinner. As concerned parents we gave her all the right instructions. Everything we did was for her own safety because we loved her and wanted to protect her. What we didn't know was that she was distraught, depressed, disillusioned, and hopeless.

As I closed the door behind me, I looked back at Sarah standing near the couch.

"Remember dinner is in the fridge. Just pop it in the microwave for a couple of minutes. I'll see you later. Bye," I said as I waved my free hand.

"Bye," she replied with a smile on her face.

That was the last time my daughter and I spoke to each other and the last time I saw her beautiful face alive.

Sarah was due to be born on June 20, 1985. Once we passed two weeks beyond the due date, the doctor was concerned, so he ran a test to be sure the baby was fine. She was. Finally, on July 8, she was born, three weeks overdue. During indescribable pain came a tiny love of my life that I longed to hold, protect, and love. Irrevocable birth. Irrevocable separation from body and unconditional connection with heart. A mother's love is a physical touch, and it's also an emotional connection that even though the umbilical cord is cut in two, the heart is never intended to be cut.

I wish I could say motherhood is all love and oohs and ahhs, but it isn't. Your little mini-me will keep you up at night, will need correction, discipline, direction, and a lot of grace. This tiny baby born through a miracle process may eventually disappoint you and even anger you. The arguments with siblings and the I-don't-want-tos will become a thorn in your side. There will be nights when they're grown that you'll pace the floor and worry about their safety and choices.

Then there will be times they make you so proud to be a mother. The beaming smile on their face when they show you the A's on their report card, the generous helping of others, and the times they hug you and won't let go.

There was no logical explanation why Sarah was three weeks late for her arrival, but God knows. He also knows why she wanted to end her life. We as a family didn't know her inward struggle. Sarah never hinted of any sort of depression or mental anguish. She was a happy, fun-loving girl with a beautiful smile that never seemed to fade. She loved to dance and sing and act silly. Inside, obviously, she was hurting and losing hope.

Perhaps you're feeling depressed and like nothing is ever going to change in your life. Maybe you're considering divorce, you've lost your job, or even lost a son or a daughter. Simply make up your mind to turn from the lies from the enemy telling you that you're not good enough. Become consistent in resisting those thoughts. Believe that the Lord will strengthen you, provide for you, and carry you in those darkened times. Spend time talking to Him and learning to know Him by spending time in His Word. Choose a trusted family member or friend and ask them to pray for you.

In Psalm 6:4–7 (NIV), King David writes,

> Turn, LORD, and deliver me; save me because of your unfailing love. Among the dead no one proclaims your name. Who praises you from the grave? I am worn out from groaning. All night long I flood my bed with weeping and drench my couch with tears. My eyes grow weak with sorrow; they fail because of all my foes.

Suddenly, David turns his thoughts from his demise and resists his foes with confidence. In the very next verses, he writes,

> Away from me, all you who do evil, for the LORD has heard my weeping. The LORD has heard my cry for mercy; the LORD accepts my prayer. All my enemies will be overwhelmed with shame and anguish; they will turn back and suddenly be put to shame. (Psalm 6:8–10 NIV)

Ah, David turned his sorrow into faith. He described how his eyes failed because of his foes, and then immediately he resisted and affirmed that the Lord accepted his prayer. And on top of that, now *his enemies* will be ashamed, not David. How awesome is *that*?

Beloved, I know it's hard. I know that you want to give up, but don't allow defeat. Rather, be determined in each step and know that the Lord of all heaven and earth *accepts* your prayer. Don't be ashamed. Lift your heart to heaven and let Him accept you just as you are—loved.

> My times are in your hands; deliver me from my enemies, from those who pursue me. Let your face shine on your servant; save me in your unfailing love. (Psalm 31:15–16 NIV)

He knows my pain and the severe shame I had held onto for so long, thinking I must've been a horrible mother if my baby didn't want to live anymore. My mind searched my memories over and over, thinking of the times I cared for her, held her tight when she didn't want to let go, and even when I spent youth camp with her.

What about when I spilled my tea on her on the way to school? And the night she left us? I could've stayed home and maybe saved her life. I wasn't there to protect her, to hold her, to tell her that everything would be okay. The weight of guilt as a mother continually bore on the side of heaviness in my soul.

Eventually over time, I came to the realization that my shame was more about what other people thought of me than what I thought of myself as a mother. Surely, I thought everyone must've thought I was a horrible mother to allow my daughter to die, and I allowed my captive thoughts to dominate me. I was too worried about what other people thought, rather than believing the truth. Then the more I reflected on my thoughts I realized this was a maneuver by the enemy to snare me into his trap of lies.

From then on, whenever Satan himself tried to steal my hand and pull me down the path to make me think I was a bad mother, I would ask God to save me and to pray for strength to stand for the truth. None of us are perfect, only God is. No one is the perfect mother or father. We learn lessons from our mistakes. My mind needed to convince itself that although I wasn't perfect, I loved her with all my heart.

I believe the magnet I bought at the gift shop at youth camp was God's message reminding me He's always with me, no matter what I'm going through. Repeatedly I have needed to believe that. The second heart is also a reminder that because I hold Sarah's memory close in my heart, she is with me, and that helps to heal my broken heart.

> The Lord is close to the brokenhearted; he rescues those whose spirits are crushed. (Psalm 34:18 NLT)

Prayer of Rescue

You are God and You are in control. When my world spins out of control, help me to remember that You have the upper hand. Help me to remember that You fight for me. And help me to remember that the words in my mind are not always Your voice and that Your plan, though different from mine sometimes, is wisdom beyond my comprehension. Thank you for Your voice of calm. In the name of the Savior, I ask these things. Amen.

CHAPTER 3

The Prayer

September 10, 1999

*A wounded soul who only shared her smile but not her pain
Just a flower in bloom that the rivers of destruction washed away too soon.*
—*Christian Joseph*

AS SOON AS RAY AND I RETURNED HOME AND WALKED IN the front door, our eyes beheld the horrific scene of our daughter lying on the floor unconscious, a gun in her hand.

I dropped my purse violently on the floor, picked up our house phone and called 911.

"Does she have a pulse?" the police dispatcher asked me.

"My God," I said in my mind, "I haven't even checked for a pulse."

I knelt, pressed my fingertips into her cold neck, and felt nothing. I knew there would be no pulse. I just knew.

"There is . . . no pulse." My voice quivered.

"There's someone on the way. Just stay on the phone with me," she said.

Then there was silence. I didn't know what to say. I didn't know what to do. I felt helpless.

I tried talking to my husband and telling him not to touch anything. He was pacing the floor in circles and flinging his arms about, his distraught voice wailing throughout the empty house. I was afraid he would smudge the murderer's fingerprints. Why I thought someone had broken into our locked home, killed my daughter, and put the gun in her right hand can only be explained as denial.

My mouth opened and words came out that I don't remember thinking.

"Are you a Christian?" I asked the dispatcher.

"Yes," she quietly said.

"Will you please pray with me?" I asked anxiously.

"I'm not allowed to, but there is a pastor's wife here in the room tonight, and I will put her on the line," she calmly replied.

The pastor's wife began to pray in a soft-spoken voice. I don't remember anything she said, but it comforted me. I still don't know who this person was, but I'm so grateful that God allowed the rules to be broken that night, allowing her to pray on the air. I wonder how many law enforcement personnel reviewed that recording and experienced God's light shining through a time of darkness. It's perplexing that the dispatcher wasn't allowed to pray but that she allowed a non-employee to be on the air and pray. It wasn't a coincidence that the pastor's wife was in the dispatch room that night. God knew beforehand what was going to take place and made it happen. There were no surprises to Him.

As I waited for the next few minutes, which felt like days, for the sheriff to arrive, I looked back at my fourteen-year-old daughter's lifeless body lying on the floor, and I thought, *Dear God, my baby is gone.* I exhaled a heavy moan that came from deep within the inmost part of my soul as a mother. I felt a physical pain in my stomach like I had been stabbed with a knife. It churned and ached. I thought I was going to vomit.

For the first few minutes after finding her lifeless body, I felt like I was inside a horrific dark cyclone. The room began to spin. A hovering darkness closed in around me. I was in a nightmarish dream with everything moving in slow motion. I couldn't move my body like normal. It was frozen in time, immovable. The weight of my arms and legs felt heavy, so much that I couldn't hardly lift them. My mind was unable to comprehend or even process what had really happened. I went into shock and became robotic in a sense.

Sarah had turned on every light in the house before positioning herself and pulling the trigger. *She must've been so afraid,* I thought. *She didn't want to be in the dark.* She had no idea darkness had already engulfed her. And now it engulfed me.

On her ninth day of ninth grade, Sarah had worn a new outfit to school. She looked so pretty. She loved that outfit. And I would never see it again after this night. It was ruined. I was ruined.

When my life drastically changed that dreadful September night, I could have run away from my relationship with God. I could have blamed Him for her decision to end her life. After all, He was the Giver of her life and now He allowed her life to be smothered to nothing, right? Let me tell you, friends, that yes, God *allows* bad things to happen, but He wants us to run *to* Him, not run *from* Him. If any of my children were suffering, I would want them to run to me for help, not run into the arms of something or someone who would immediately satisfy their longing. I would have died for any of my children in order that they wouldn't be hurt. I'm a protector of whom I love, and that's what God is for each one of us.

When Sarah was a young girl, she would hold on to me. It started as a hug and turned into playing and tickling fun because she didn't ever want to let go. She giggled as I tickled her, and then when I went to get up to go cook dinner, she wouldn't let go as she slowly slid her body all the way down to my ankles. Both of us still laughing, I struggled to pull her along, her hands locked onto my ankles as I made my way to the kitchen. I have to admit she was strong. I affectionately called her my little leech, one who hung on and wouldn't let go. She held on as I kept walking and wouldn't let go until finally her sister came along and tickled her. Then the chase was on. Off to their bedroom they ran, grasping at walls, laughing, pretty much stumbling over each other, racing to make it to the bed first, as though that was the finish line or safety zone.

Over the years I've often wondered if Sarah hung on to me because she was afraid. Or because she needed me. Maybe she desired love more because she needed more reassurance that she was loved.

I can't continue trying to solve all the whys and what-ifs. I can only reflect on the memories of the times we hugged, played, laughed, and loved.

There have been times in my grief when I was confused because I thought that God didn't protect Sarah, but as I've learned in my walk with Him, Sarah's death was the work of the enemy of all evil. Apparently, she believed his lies that her life wasn't worth living. She was drowning in a river of lies and didn't know how to pull herself out. She could've reached out to someone but didn't. Not one human person knew how Sarah felt. Friends, family, no one. But God did. Oh, how I wish she would've reached out to the Giver of life and prayed to be rescued.

So many times in life I could have avoided fear, worry, anger, and heartache if only I had called on His name. Have you ever felt that way? In my early Christian walk, I didn't realize how powerful prayer really was. I think a lot of the time we lack the faith to believe that God *will* answer. That He'll replace our fear with faith. That He'll give us trust in Him, so we don't have to worry. That He'll calm us and give us peace in the middle of the storm where anger dwells. And that He'll provide the faithful love to mend the heartache we feel.

We wrestle with what to say and how we can say it so eloquently like the pastor who prays from the podium Sunday mornings. We don't have to wrestle. It doesn't have to be a perfect prayer with many words. Simple prayers will do. Words can flow from the heart as you call His name. A small, gentle whisper of the name, Jesus. Again, Jesus. And once more, Jesus. You'll begin to feel comfort and peace. Then simply talk to Him like He's your friend. We need to remain respectful and recognize the holiness of the ground we stand on in His presence. But we also need to remember He's a friend of ours like He was a friend to His disciples. Whisper the name of the greatest friend you've ever had, and you'll find rest. It might be a peaceful moment. It might be a powerful moment. In either case, He will give you rest as you seek His presence.

Come to me, all you who are weary and burdened, and I will give you rest. Take my yoke upon you and learn from me, for I am gentle and humble in heart, and you will find rest for your souls. (Jesus speaking, Matthew 11:28–29 NIV)

Other times, we may feel weak and don't know how or what to pray for, but the Holy Spirit joins us and groans for us and helps us.

Likewise, the Spirit helps us in our weakness. For we do not know what to pray for as we ought, but the Spirit himself intercedes for us with groanings too deep for words. (Romans 8:26 ESV)

At night when I'm lying in bed trying to clear my mind of the day's cluttered thoughts, I don't quite have the words to say, but I release a sigh with a gentle groan. Have you ever done that? I feel the weight of the day's struggles and load of stress, and a groan comes out. A sigh. A cry for help. My groan reminds me of a little girl lost in the dark woods who doesn't know her way home. She's lost and overwhelmed. She's frightened and hears strange sounds. Her heart is racing, she's sweating, and her eyes are darting back and forth, not knowing which direction to run home.

The groan is a call. It's a way to reach out to God for rescue. It's a hand reached to heaven with a longing for the Father to reach down and grab me out of the deep waters I have fallen into. It is in my weakness that He is strong. And He steps up, just as His Word says.

But He (Jesus) said to me, "My grace is sufficient for you, for my power is made perfect in weakness." (2 Corinthians 12:9a NIV)

So, when we are weak, His power excels. Capture that promise right there. Not that we ever want to be weak, but in the times that we are, He is there. He is listening. He wants to become more powerful to each one of us if we'll let Him. A power that is made perfect.

For years I thought of my daughter's death as a weakness. The written definition of weakness is "the state or condition of lacking strength" or "a quality or feature regarded as a disadvantage or fault."[1] There is an empty space in my heart because she is gone, but it doesn't reflect on me as a weakness. Ever so gradually, the Lord has shown me that when I feel the cup of my soul is empty, He fills it to overflowing with blessings, with faithfulness and mercy, and with unconditional love. He now fills that empty space, that void, to overflowing.

You see, it's okay not to feel strong all the time. It's okay if we feel weak. It's okay not to be perfect. It's okay that we don't have to carry so much weight on our shoulders. It's okay that when we don't know what to pray, the Holy Spirit groans for us and gives us rest.

As Paul goes on to write, "For when I am weak, then I am strong" (2 Corinthians 12:10 NIV).

Prayer of Rest

Father God, You are the might and strength of heaven and earth, and it is in the times of my weakness that I need You the most. Fill my groanings with Your rest. Calm every wave of circumstance that frightens me, Lord. Thank You for the privilege of prayer. It's in the strong name of Jesus that I pray. Amen.

---

1 "Weakness" definition, Dictionary.com.

CHAPTER 4

The Peace

September 10, 1999

Together, forever, that's how we'll always be
No longer will I see the sadness
Since you brought my life happiness
Now you're a part of me.
—Sarah Cullison

ONCE THE SHERIFF ARRIVED AFTER FINDING SARAH, RAY and I weren't allowed back into our home. We stood outside in the darkness, a darkness I had never felt so enveloped in as I did that night. The night was black. The only light that arrayed our entire street was the red and blue rotating lights from the police cars that surrounded our home. Several police officers went in and out of our front door, and I felt helpless. I longed to be with my daughter, my baby girl, to hold her hand, to whisper in her ear that everything was going to be okay, but I couldn't. My home, and my daughter, were now considered a crime scene.

Ray called several people trying to find our son Raymond who was at the high school football game. Eventually, Ray reached someone who was able to locate Raymond in the crowd.

When Raymond pulled in near our house, we quickly walked to the street to meet him. We told him what had happened to Sarah.

Raymond stepped back, after we embraced for a moment, and asked excitedly, "What?" Then his eyes were filled with disbelief. He stretched out his arms. He cried, "Why? Why?"

In the midst of my own sobbing, I said, "I don't know. I don't know." There was no consoling him. I stood there with a distance between us as though we were separated by an empty mass in the atmosphere. I couldn't calm him. It was heart-wrenching as a mother, but I had to let him grieve his sister's loss.

We called our daughter Namantha's employer, and they told her to come home because of an emergency. She pulled up in her car and hurriedly walked up to Ray and I. When Ray told her that her sister had taken her own life, Namantha collapsed to the ground on her knees, tears streaming down her face.

I felt utterly helpless. I couldn't console my children as they mourned. They had to release the emotions first. Our tears wouldn't stop. I could hardly catch my breath.

Ray paced the yard making phone calls telling family and friends the bad news. I couldn't. Just the thought of having to tell someone that my daughter took her own life made me feel ill. The pit of my stomach felt like someone inside stirring hot porridge round and round. The emotions of anxiety, sadness, confusion, frustration, and helplessness swirled around in my head, and all I could do to release them was walk back and forth across our small front yard.

I wanted to get in my car and leave and drive and drive and drive. I wanted to run away. But at the same time, the longing I felt was to stay there with her because my little girl was inside and I thought she needed me. Although only her body was left behind, there was no possibility I could ever leave her. I felt attached to her but detached at the same time. It didn't make any sense. None of this made sense. I felt like I was living inside a dream. No, not a dream. A nightmare.

As I stood outside, I looked up at the dark sky. The moon hung in the sky and the stars still shone, but my light had been snuffed out. The limbs of my body felt weighted like a tree had fallen on me. I had energy that I didn't know what to do with. It was anxiety, an emotion that was my constant escort. My body began to convulse as though I had the chills. It was a warm night, so it wasn't the cold. My body had begun to go into shock.

Awhile later that night, a friend and pastor lady friend came to comfort us. I had already been questioning God and how He played a part in this. Their hugs were welcomed. My temporary world that had spun out of whack suddenly became familiar again seeing them.

"Please tell me that God didn't do this," I pleaded to the pastor.

She replied, "Oh yes, my dear, God didn't do this. This is the work of the enemy."

That reassurance comforted me for a moment. I didn't want to lose God over this. I didn't want to think that a child of mine (and a child of His) had died a violent death because of Him. At least I had the enemy to blame. My faith became immature in an instant. My thoughts and emotions burst out of me like a prisoner bursting loose from his chains. My self-control spun completely out of control. My shy, introverted self didn't think first and hold my tongue. I flung words out without filtering them through my mind first.

A couple of hours later, the sheriff suggested we leave for the night. A married couple and good friends, Bill and Hannah, came and drove us to their home. The silence in the car wrenched at me as we drove through the black night. I didn't want to leave our home. I didn't want to leave my baby girl. I wanted to see her body safely transported somewhere else. I wanted to stay all night. I wanted to wait until the sun rose in the morning and then I would feel better, knowing this was all a dream. The longing in my chest ached so badly that it was physically painful.

Once we settled in, Ray and I crawled into bed to try and get some sleep. We held each other like we had never held each other before. We were scared, intimidated by our new surroundings, even though we were comfortable with our friends. We tried turning the light off but turned it back on. We were still restless, so we turned the light off again. We could hardly close our eyes, even in the dark. We were too far flung into darkness already. We tossed and turned. There was no forgetting what we saw, what we experienced. The only momentary comfort we found was in each other's arms.

We finally dozed off to sleep around 4:00 a.m. for maybe an hour. Voices woke me. I heard Ray and Bill talking. I smelled coffee brewing and heard the clicking sound of their dog's nails walking on the tile. It was morning. The next day. The first day after.

Oh, dear God, what has happened? Do I have to face this day? I thought.

In the days that followed, the people of our small town of Kingman, Arizona, flooded us with phone calls, visits, food, and cards. Several cards a day came in the mail with encouraging words and money in them. Almost every card contained money. My Dad said, "Never in my whole life have I ever seen so many cards and money come in because of a loss in a family." He shook his head in disbelief.

I knew in my heart that God was with us, comforting us, providing for us. He was showing us that He's for us, not against us.

Ray called a meeting between us and our two kids. Raymond was now nineteen years old and Namantha was almost eighteen. As we walked across the lawn in my parents' backyard, I was reminded of how many family gatherings, holidays, and laughter filled this space at various times over the years. Today Raymond and Namantha weren't playing tag or Red Light, Green Light, or football with their cousins.

Raymond was almost as tall as Ray now, an adult, handsome with those gifted blue eyes. His hair had darkened as he grew older, and he kept it cut short. He was now working in the health field full time. Namantha had just started her senior year in high school, very disciplined in her study and grades. As she walked in front of me, her long brown hair blew in the wind, and she turned around, her profile displaying the beauty of her face, to make sure I was still coming. It was ironic that Namantha, Sarah, and I all had the same hair color.

As we walked across the yard to my parents' travel trailer near the back gate, I knew the purpose of our family meeting was to discuss and plan Sarah's funeral service. God's purpose for that hour was much more than that.

When I closed the trailer door with only the four of us inside, this was a moment of truth. The heart of our family, minus one, was in this room alone together. I felt close to my husband and children, and yet there was a void, a missing element. It was Sarah. We all felt it. Raymond and Namantha's eyes were easily looking to the floor with sadness. Their cheeks weren't active with smiles. Their eyes were inquisitive about this meeting yet somehow reflected that they knew this needed to be done.

Ray explained to our kids that he knew there would be emotions of grief we would experience. He knew because eighteen years earlier, his mother had taken her own life. He had traveled this road of grief before.

"This is going to either make us as a family or break us as a family," he warned gently.

"You're right," Raymond agreed.

"Yes," Namantha said, shaking her head in agreement.

"We're going to experience anger, frustration, even depression. We have to remember that we need to be patient and understanding with each other."

Wow, how true. How profound. For such a time as this for those words to come out, the wisdom in those words were needed. We all decided that this loss, this devastation, this tragedy was going to make us as a family. We grew closer together, and my faith grew stronger in that moment.

During this time, many were praying for us. Our church, the youth group, many pastors, many family members, and many friends. We felt them. Although the nights were dark, my hope was helped a little with each sunrise. I knew I would find comfort in praying and reading the Bible, so I made it a point, without fail, to start every day this way. I then felt His presence. I felt peace. I felt promise for a new day.

> O dear friend, when thy grief presses thee to the very dust, worship there.
>
> —Charles Spurgeon[2]

---

2 Charles Spurgeon, *www.spurgeon.org*, *"Job's Resignation" (MTP 42, Sermon 2457, p 134).*

In the days that followed, Ray and I ran errands and took care of matters for the funeral service. I wasn't looking forward to the errands and the appointments for all the arrangements. We walked outside to the car, the warm sunshine landed on my face, greeting me with a breath of hope, a good feeling that things may not always stay cold and dark in my world.

I dreaded facing people. I didn't want to be seen and put on a smile to be cordial. As we walked into each building to handle matters, I slipped my hand into Ray's. His strong hand gripped mine firmly, and I found comfort. God provides other ways to help in those times our faith weakens.

Some days my faith wasn't as strong as others. There were bad days where I just wanted to be in heaven and not face this horrible demise for the rest of my years. Grief is a door that we have no choice but to walk through, an onset of emotions that actually helps to get us through the process. Every small step from the nightfall at the end of one day into the sunrise of the next was the key to survival.

I confess I was afraid, afraid to close my eyes, afraid to sleep, afraid to be in the dark, afraid of what tomorrow would bring. In my mind's eye, I was on a boat in the middle of the ocean with the winds howling and the boat rocking. Water rushed in. The oars are lost, nowhere to be seen. I'm stranded in the middle of nowhere, feeling alone and panicking. I hear no boat horns. I see no lights in the distance. I'm lost at sea and I'm failing. I feel weaker until I feel like I can't hold on anymore. I need to signal SOS. In my despair I desperately call out His name. A life preserver is then tossed my way, and I pull it toward me and put it around me. My faith begins to rise above the fear.

Our lives may never be the same following a major loss, but clutching to faith will see us through. Faith that God will carry us through another day and that we will be there for each other. What is necessary in times of struggle and loss is believing that a rescue will come.

I realize sometimes faith is hard. We want to work it out on our own, don't we? We want to listen to other ways of feeling better, worldly ways. We want to make other things our life buoy, but it's not the right way.

Jesus calmed my horrific ocean. He made a way and that way was the cross. He faced rejection, shame, bloodshed, and was crucified on the cross and died for you and for me. He chose to be our Life-Saver and sacrificed His safety for us. If we let go of faith in Him, we may slip back into the darkness and the danger. Let go of your struggle and hold tight to your faith.

> Now faith is confidence in what we hope for and assurance about what we do not see. (Hebrews 11:1 NIV)

Prayer of Faith

Father, I lay myself down and worship You for who You are. You are the Giver of faith, and I pray in those dark moments that You will show Your faithfulness to me in a way that only I can understand. Increase Your grace, I pray, so that faith prevails. It is in the faithful name of Jesus that I ask this. Amen.

CHAPTER 5

The Forgiveness

September 12, 1999

You made me see what I didn't know before
I'm glad I let you come through my door
The door that opened my heart; that was to love you,
Now I know things I never knew.
—Sarah Cullison

IT WAS SUNDAY, SEPTEMBER 12, 1999, AND FAMILY HAD GATH-
ered to be together at my parents' house. A few visitors came and gave
their condolences and then shortly left. The smaller kids played outside
in the backyard. The sun was shining, the grass was green, the warmth
of the day reminded us that soon winter would be here.

Ray and I were sitting in the backyard when two visitors, a former
boyfriend of Sarah and his mother, walked around the corner of the
house from the side yard. After introductions, the four of us stood
around the deck of the patio, and there the conversation became an
epitome of forgiveness.

The young boy explained how he felt that Sarah taking her life
was all his fault. Here stood a fourteen-year-old boy, a popular high
schooler, humbled and overcome with guilt. His mother told us that
they were afraid to come because they thought sure we would retaliate
and blame him for the death of our daughter. *My sweet Lord.*

"What kind of Christian would I be to blame you for what
my daughter did, just to ease my pain?" Ray said. Wise words, very
wise words.

The young man's eyes flooded tears of relief. I could tell the weight of the world fell from his shoulders. His mother gently put her arm around him, reassuring him that everything would be all right. What torture and mockery he must have faced from other students for months at school. I prayed this boy would not give up.

Ray said in his defense, "If these kids keep beating you up this way, I'll call the principal of the school and arrange an assembly. I'll speak to them and tell them that what they're doing is wrong."

We hugged him just as tight as we could that day. Not just because he came to apologize and possibly thought he may have to face ridicule, but because he meant something to our little girl. Maybe in her innocence, he was her reason for living. And because of that, we loved him too.

He told us he received a letter in the mail from Sarah. My heart sank. Three days before as Sarah and I ran through the drop-off box at the post office, I didn't think much about her sending a letter. I just thought that with the school year starting, maybe she didn't have any classes with him and wouldn't see him. I wanted to read the note furiously to find out why my daughter felt there was nothing left in the world to live for, but I had to be patient. He had already given it to the police. We finally received the letter from the police a few days later. It started sweet and happy. Then turned very angry as she shared her pain and hurt. Sarah felt betrayed and useless. She closed with her goodbyes and that was the end.

Sarah had forgotten. She had forgotten the purpose of life, the zeal for life, the laughter with friends, the love of family. In her time of loss, she had forgotten us. She had forgotten me, the one person in her life who carried her, held her, tickled her, helped her, cared for her, loved her. And she had forgotten about God, the One who loved her most.

So little is said when suicide is involved. After all, it's such an ugly word. In days of old, no one talked about it. The subject and even the person who died was swept beneath everyday greetings in every conversation. We now remember the person taken as the kind, loving person they were. And somehow when we think that they were depressed, desperate, with no hope, we wonder why. To envision that person either hanging themselves, jumping off a bridge, or shooting themselves is a picture we don't want to think about. It's desperation, an abnormal state of mind.

Suicide is the nation's second leading cause of death in fifteen- to twenty-four-year-olds. Most are too young to even comprehend the extent of their decision. Perhaps some are too young to want to live any longer because they can't see any change or improvement in their future lives. They are so far deep in waters of their hopelessness that they see no hope for a cure. Some are in seemingly hopeless situations such as divorce or bankruptcy and see no way out. And some, if not all, feel unloved.

I don't believe anyone entirely understands suicide. Psychiatrists and even medical doctors speculate to explain the whys, but unless someone survives an attempt, we may never understand it from an individual basis, and even then, the living victim may not divulge all of their emotions.

The evil and darkness of it all is frightening and intimidating, to say the least. I have read studies on suicide and attended training and listened to testimonials from suicide attempt victims. For many, their beliefs about themselves are the biggest factor. They feel they're a failure, not attractive, alone, and even a hindrance.

I believe suicide is one of the strongest tools yet that the enemy uses to destroy lives. Not just the ones that end their lives, but for those left behind. Shame, anger, depression, blame, and guilt can play a part in the lives of those who survive the suicide of a friend or family member. We are the survivors. We are the ones left behind who must decide whether we are going to succumb to these same symptoms ourselves or whether we are going to speak up against it and fight this ugly war.

Those of us family and friends who have survived the loss of a loved one by suicide are left with emotions we initially don't know what to do with. Becoming angry with the victim and even with God are instinctive reactions we come face to face with. We try reasoning with one another. What was wrong with him or her? Was she suffering from a mental illness? How could she do this? Why would she do this to *us*? It quickly can become anger toward the victim. Like any other emotion, let me encourage you to try to forgive that person. We need forgiveness for our own selves, mentally *and* physically.

Often in my grief walk, I questioned God.

"Why did you let this happen?"

"How could you let this happen?"

"I thought you were a good God, but you allowed evil to destroy my little girl."

"Where were you?"

"Why didn't you rescue her?"

"Will you make this all go away?"

"Will you rescue *me*?"

To let go of my anger, I needed to forgive Sarah and I needed to forgive God. Most of the time I clung to God to save me, but in weak moments, I ran from Him, thinking I could escape Him and what He allowed to happen. It wasn't long before I realized running away only caused me more suffering. He was my Healer, but I had become an impediment. Soon I realized my life was so much better with Him in it. I leaned on Him when I felt tired. Even in the times I felt ashamed, I found worth in Him because I knew He accepted me. I found rest when I felt guilty. I didn't have to wrestle with anxiety constantly. I had to surrender it all.

In the weeks after Sarah's death, Ray and I both wrestled with unforgiveness.

One particular morning we were sitting at the dining-room table after breakfast.

"Yesterday I was really struggling," Ray said, clutching his coffee cup.

I placed my hand on his forearm. "I'm sorry, honey."

"So, I took my Bible and opened it and as the pages fell open, I just started reading 2 Corinthians," he said, resisting tears.

"Yeah, what did it say?" I asked.

"Go get your Bible and let's read it together."

I turned to 2 Corinthians. Ray pointed to verse 2 and said, "Here, start reading here."

> If anyone has caused grief, he has not so much grieved me as he has grieved all of you to some extent—not to put it too severely. The punishment inflicted on him by the majority is sufficient. Now instead, you ought to forgive and comfort him, so that he will not be overwhelmed by excessive sorrow. I urge you, therefore, to reaffirm your love for him. Another reason I wrote you was to see if you would stand the test and be obedient in everything. Anyone you forgive, I also forgive. And what I have forgiven—if there was anything to forgive—I have forgiven in the sight of Christ for your sake, in order that Satan might not outwit us. For we are not unaware of his schemes. (2 Corinthians 2:5–11 NIV)

I leaned back in my chair, astounded by the message.

"When I read this, I knew I needed to forgive Sarah for what she did," Ray confessed.

Ray had been angry at Sarah, and the Scripture spoke to him that he needed to forgive her. Not just for her, but for him too. When we don't let go of unforgiveness, it's usually because we just don't want to. Somehow it makes us feel good being angry. We believe that we deserve to be angry and that the person we're angry at deserves every emotion boiling from that anger. What we need to be careful *not* to do is sin when we're angry. Unleashing hurtful words on someone else to make ourselves feel better only damages and doesn't heal.

Healing is linked to forgiveness.[3]

—Corrie ten Boom, Christian author

Continuing to be stuck in the rut of unforgiveness can destroy us and certainly won't heal our hurts. Just as a ship is pushed out to sea

---

3 Corrie ten Boom with Jamie Buckingham, *Tramp for the Lord* (London: Hodder and Stoughton, 1975), 217–218.

by the waves from the shoreline, we can gradually be taken out farther and farther into the sea of unforgiveness. Soon we find ourselves alone, being slapped by the waves of angry reminders that continue to float around us like driftwood along our captivity. We become a castaway, a lonely, lost soul searching for delivery back to normality.

Unfortunately, our culture today has somehow established that being unforgiving is justified, deserving, and self-gratifying, and that forgiveness is a weakness. But it's quite the contrary. Mastering forgiveness isn't always easy, but it is attainable. You may struggle fighting forgiveness like a boat being tossed by giant waves on a storm at sea as I did until I finally realized that resisting forgiveness was taking my strength away, depriving me of healing. Let me encourage you that persevering through the struggle of forgiveness will produce growth in you and strength in your struggle and will also bring healing.

Imagine a small seed beneath the surface of the ground. It has to push through pounds of dirt in order to bust through the surface and reach sunshine. It's the same with our emotional health. In order to reach the other side where there is freedom, we have to push through the struggle and forgive.

When it seems like you may be lost at sea, drowning in despair in the sea of emotions, it's hard to see the light in the distance. But there is a lighthouse shining from shore to shore, beckoning to come where it's safe. The Lord is that lighthouse for you even though you seem surrounded by fog and unfamiliarity. Don't be afraid. Rush to shore toward the lighthouse, and into the arms of the One who loves you no matter how you feel. In His presence there is a peace that by human form we can't explain, but it is available at no cost.

Something as simple as a smile from someone you meet can provide healing after a traumatic event or a gradual heartbreak. If a friend needs a candle to shine in their darkness, be present and allow them to talk as you listen. Sharing is therapeutic and helps those of us who have lost someone. We love to talk about them, to share memories. There doesn't have to be a lot of words said. Sometimes an overabundance of words of advice we think are helpful can actually be hurtful to the grieving person, although unintentional. The following simple phrases can be very helpful. "I'm sorry you have to go through this. I'm just a phone call away if you need someone," or "I can't imagine how you feel, but I'll always be here for you," or "I'll never forget them, and I'll never forget you." It's okay to tell someone grieving that you're there for them and that you're there to listen. Or just share a hug. Sometimes it's better when words are not even spoken. We can read each other's facial expressions and body language and know that the person needs reassurance that everything's going to be okay.

Please don't use these words:

"At least they're no longer suffering." Because now you are.

"Well, now they're in a better place." But now you're not.

These types of phrases don't help the grieving person because these words don't encourage them in the midst of their suffering.

Rather, the following words can be comforting:

"I'm always here for you."

"What can I do to help?"

"What would you like to do today?"

"Can I take you to lunch?"

"I'm ready to listen when you're ready to talk."

There are also physical ways that can help in the healing process. Music is very powerful. After Sarah died, happy music helped me some days. Other days it just didn't fit. And some days soft, slow ballads were a healing balm.

Going for walks helped me to release anxiety also. Do something that works for you. It might be a workout or cooking or being with family. For us grandparents, being with our grandchildren helped. Watching a funny movie helped us because for a few minutes we were engulfed in laughter and it was okay. Also, being outdoors brings fresh air and a new outlook on life. Ray and I like to go on ATV rides. It's so beautiful looking at the beauty of our desert landscapes and the sunsets. The wonderful smells from the cedar bushes and pine trees emit a breath of fresh air as well.

And of course, animals can lift our spirits. Just being around a dog or cat or any other animal that loves to be around you can turn depression into happiness. Amazingly enough, we are the ones who love on them by petting them and they are the ones that give us joy. Funny, isn't it?

It's all about life. The biggest gift we have is life, and we need to enjoy living it. There may be good days and there may be bad days, yes, but the joys of life are worth having and appreciating. That, my friend, is healing.

> Be kind and compassionate to one another, forgiving each other, just as in Christ God forgave you. (Ephesians 4:32 NIV)

Prayer of Forgiveness

Lord, show me the areas where I need to forgive. I confess it's hard for me to forgive, and yet I know it's what I need to do. Thank you for forgiving me for mistakes I've made. Help me to release feelings of bitterness and betrayal toward others. Make me into a foreshadow of You by being kind and forgiving. In the healing name of Jesus I pray. Amen.

CHAPTER 6

The Funeral

September 15, 1999

We know that we will hold her in our arms again someday,
So we'll try to move on,
And never live our lives as though all hope is gone.
—Christian Joseph

THE DREADED DAY HAD FINALLY ARRIVED. FUNERAL DAY.
For the last five days, there had been a constant flow of visitors and
flowers and food, but today, for the ceremony honoring my daughter,
it all came to a halt. A screeching halt, with silence. A deafening silence.
It seemed the world stopped spinning, and there was nothing left but
abandon in the hollow depth of grief.

I didn't want to face this day. All of the arrangements, all of the
appointments could just go away as far as I was concerned. It wasn't
as if I didn't want to honor my little girl. I did. I just didn't want this
day to happen because if it didn't happen, I wouldn't have to face it.

The service wasn't until three o'clock in the afternoon, so we had
to face several hours of anxiety. With every passing minute, I felt my
heartbeat increase. My hands shook. My legs were weak and wobbly.
I stumbled just walking from room to room. I felt someone had a large
stirring spoon pushing everything around inside of me in all different
directions.

I went outside into the cool morning, and I noticed in the sky
that clouds were moving in above me. *Of course,* I thought, *that this*
would turn out to be a cloudy, dreary day. I took a long, deep breath
to help relieve the anxiety that I felt someone stuffed down inside of

57

me like they were packing supplies for a year. I hated it. I hated not being able to breathe. I hated my mind constantly racing, unable to focus. I hated this day. I never thought I would ever have to face a day like today. I dreaded it.

"God, please help me. I need You," I pleaded.

Ray and I managed to shower, get dressed, and eat a little something while receiving what seemed like a hundred phone calls. I wore the pretty purple dress that Hannah had bought me. I wondered if the short length was really appropriate for my daughter's service. I shrugged off that feeling of inadequacy. It was too late to change now.

The flowers had been ordered for the casket, the pastors had prepared their words, the church members had food prepared and ready to feed the guests. All of the music had been arranged. We had arranged our kids to meet us at the church, the church where I had attended, grown, and served with joy. I determined there would be no joy today.

We got in our car and headed for the church about fifteen minutes away. There wasn't much to say between us. We had talked about everything. There was the silence again. I never thought in my life that we would be driving to our daughter's funeral. Ever. I could feel my pulse in my neck. I grabbed my husband's hand and we squeezed our fingers together. I was so thankful I had him with me. I didn't want to face this day at all, but I was so thankful I had someone to cling to, someone to lean on, someone who understood.

When we pulled into the church parking lot, there were so many cars there that I didn't see one parking space empty. I had thought there might be a small crowd, but never guessed there would be this many people. We had the viewing the day before at the funeral home with a constant flow of people for a couple hours. So many of her friends came and sat and watched. And cried. And held each other. Over a thousand people said their goodbyes. Our church, which held approximately three hundred and fifty people, was unprepared for this many people. So was I. As I slid on my sunglasses, I thought I could slip into the crowd, unnoticed. Slim chance.

One of the two pastors conducting the service met us at the side entrance to the sanctuary and courteously escorted us to our seats on the front row. The spacious room was already full of people. Ushers had to set up extra chairs on the platform where the musicians and pastor normally speak from. As more people came, the ushers asked people to stand along the walls, and there still wasn't enough room. I'm sure the building fire code was graciously displaced that day. The helpers even moved speakers outside so the crowd standing outside could hear. We were overwhelmed with the support from our little town.

Before the service started, a light rain started to fall. The sun was shining, and the rain still fell, slow, big drops of rain. The procession began of the pallbearers accompanying Sarah's body from the hearse into the sanctuary. Just as they pulled her casket out of the car, the rain stopped, and they proceeded to the sanctuary. The moment the back end of the casket made its way into the doorway, the rain started again.

The casket spread that laid across the top of Sarah's casket was yellow and pink roses. They were beautiful.

If only Sarah could see them, I thought to myself.

We chose yellow because that was Sarah's favorite color. A color representing sunshine. And we chose pink because she was our little girl, even still at fourteen years old. It was a beautiful combination of color with a touch of green leaves and white baby's breath. Sarah's casket was a light rose color, but what convinced us to choose this one was the pastel pink interior and the rose that appeared on the inside of the top lid. It was perfect for our little girl.

Fourteen different families had donated rose bushes to decorate around the casket, representing each year of Sarah's life. There were seven rose bushes with all yellow roses, and then there were seven rose bushes with all pink roses. Fourteen families. The staff at the church didn't turn away the fifteenth family because there wasn't one to turn away. Fourteen years was Sarah's life. It's ironic that exactly fourteen were donated. Seven yellow and seven pink. How can this be a coincidence?

I kept reiterating in my thoughts, *Pink and yellow. Pink and yellow. Why did those colors seem so familiar to me?* Later I realized why those colors were so prevalent. Pink and yellow were the colors of the bridesmaid's dresses at our wedding. Another coincidence? Impossible.

The beautiful aroma that emitted the area surrounding Sarah's coffin reached us family members who were seated close on the front row. I loved that the fragrance of such delicate beauty surrounded the resting place of a beautiful, tender heart.

Our former pastor's voice pelted from the podium to open the service and pulled me out of my mind wanderings. He opened the service with a short message on the emotions we expected to experience and how to persevere through them.

Not more than two weeks before this, Sarah had performed with three other girls in our youth group, signing the song *Shout to the Lord*. My mind wandered to the memory of that day. I remember Sarah standing on that stage, performing with the other girls, and I was so proud. At that time I didn't know her body would be lying in a casket a few feet away just days later.

To honor her sister, Namantha learned the song also and beautifully performed it at the funeral with one of Sarah's friends, Judy. I knew Namantha was nervous. She glanced over at me, and I smiled to encourage her that she can do this. The two girls waited for the music to begin, Judy in her short, dark hair and big bell-bottom pants, and Namantha across the stage in her pretty burgundy and black dress.

During the song Namantha lifted her arm as part of the signing. It was then she started to weep as she held her hand toward heaven with her eyes closed, tears streaming down her face. Oh, how my heart ached with my little girl in that moment of sad passion. I longed to run and hold her in my arms, but I couldn't. Not until the song was done.

The pastor of our church shared a message on salvation and opened the gospel of Jesus to the hundreds of people inside the building and those standing outside. Two people I know of openly confessed that day and received Christ in their hearts. A painful day had become a day of glorious renewal for two souls and maybe more we don't know of. Several pastors from area churches had attended to help with counseling.

Family and friends shared stories about Sarah. Some were sad and some were funny. My face was so red from the constant falling of tears, yet it helped my heart. It helped to remember her and to talk about her. Some shared how Sarah was an encourager and had the most beautiful smile. She helped those with sadness. She just couldn't help her own.

As the service ended, the pallbearers accompanied Sarah's casket back to the vehicle. The second the head of the casket crossed the threshold of the church doors, it stopped raining again. And for the long, slow walk back to the hearse, the rain halted until the casket was pushed into the back of the car. The drops started again. Could it be a sign that God was sad with us? After all, Sarah wasn't just our child. She was His.

There were over two thousand people there at Sarah's funeral that day. Some standing in the rain and some standing with nowhere to sit for over two hours. For her. For us. For each other. For another hour we stood in the fellowship hall greeting person after person. Some brought food. Some brought hugs. Some brought tears. The guests who came hurting the worst, and ones I clung to, were those who had cared for her. Babysitters. And her friends. Even though I hardly knew some of her friends, I felt I had a connection with them that is unexplainable. A love that delves so deep no one can understand is a love like this.

As the sun began to set on the day of Sarah's service and the crowds had pretty much dissipated except for family, we were able to sit and sigh with relief. We talked about funny things Sarah did and funny things we all did. The room echoed with laughter and I welcomed it. Although my mind was inundated with everyone there, through the words spoken and the hugs given, my shoulders didn't feel so weighted down. I was able to take a deep breath and sigh.

We took pictures of family outside in front of the sunset. The sun was barely peeking over the horizon and the sky emitted a soft mixture of orange and blue. Everyone looked happy, warmed by their arms around each other. Smiles shown like the sun. Everyone looked relieved, glad this day was over. So was I.

So many times I said to myself, *I can't believe this happened to me.* I felt like a failure as a mother. I felt I must've been a horrible mother to let this happen to my child. Yes, I could have been better, but the accuser, the enemy who hates me, whispered in my ear these evil accusations and I accepted them. I believed them. I accepted the false punishment.

As the pastor mentioned, among all the emotions we experience, death brings with it a plethora of emotions and sometimes all at once. Depression, loneliness, anxiety, guilt, shame, regret, and more.

The constant struggle with the emotions of grief reminded me of how Jesus must have felt before He was crucified. It is written in Matthew 26:37 that in the garden of Gethsemane, He felt sorrowful and troubled. In verse 38, Jesus indicated His soul was overwhelmed with sorrow to the point of death. In verse 38, He said to his disciples, "Stay here and keep watch with me" (Matthew 26:38 NIV). I imagine He was also feeling lonely, and that's why He asked Peter and the others to stay with Him.

Then he fell with his face to the ground and prayed. He was overburdened, overwhelmed, overwrought, and dreading his demise. There were three times He went away and prayed, the first two times pleading with the Lord that this cup be taken from Him. Have you ever prayed for something and then again and again? Could it be He needed to pray all three times in order to submit to God's plan? I know I've struggled with that before as well.

Later on in Matthew, the chief priests and the elders of the people came to arrest Jesus, led by Judas, one of his disciples. Judas indicated who Jesus was by kissing him. Imagine this. You have a follower, a friend, a man who listened to your teachings and witnessed healing by your own hand, and now he is turning you over to your enemies with a kiss no less.

Verse 56 reads, "Then all the disciples deserted him and fled." Possibly they ran away, snuck away, or slithered into the crowd and disappeared. I know when I am experiencing the most horrific moment of my life, if my friends were to betray and desert me, there's no doubt once the dust settled that I would feel alone and betrayed.

As Jesus stood before Caiaphas, the high priest, and teachers of the law and elders, He was accused of blasphemy. Jesus remained silent. And once He professed to be the Son of God, they spit in his face and beat him with their fists. The chief priests and the whole Sanhedrin were looking to put Jesus to death, even with false evidence, but none was found. Even the truth He spoke was challenged.

Has anyone ever accused you of something you didn't do? It's humiliating and makes me feel angry when they are so convinced I have done something false. Naturally I defend myself and try to explain the truth. But Jesus didn't do that. He stayed silent. Why do you suppose He wouldn't defend himself? Would it worsen His sentence? I don't think so. You can't get much worse than a death sentence. Jesus remained calm. We tend to believe He didn't resist when He was beaten but was meek and gentle, wise and strong. By standing by His belief and not engaging their ridicule, He appeared to them to be weak. But He was strong. He knew the Father was watching. He knew the Lord, who could have called legions of angels, was with Him. He knew the enemy dwelled in these accusers and would one day either face their own pathetic demise or feel remorse and change their hearts toward the truth.

The Word doesn't tell us what Jesus was thinking. It simply tells the story itself. The Lord has left it to our imaginations to think for ourselves. He gives us that choice. He doesn't force Himself on us, nor does He reject us if we don't first believe. He simply waits. And so did Jesus.

Matthew goes on to tell us they slapped Jesus and mocked Him. Likely on His knees on rock in the warm sun, blood dripped from Jesus onto the ground. Surely His body ached. His blood pressure rose. Sweat mingled with blood. His body grew weaker. But He didn't. He remained steadfast and didn't try to escape. He didn't call ten thousand angels to release him and didn't beg for mercy. He simply accepted the false punishment.

I was now faced with accepting the false punishment of my daughter's death. When I didn't want to go on, when I didn't want to face other people's judgment, and when I just wanted to pretend this didn't happen, there was only one thing to do.

I had to push myself to persevere.

Are you faced today with what seems like a hopeless situation in your life and don't know where to turn? Are you wanting to just give up? The rooted dark troubles that exist way down into the deep well of our souls may seem too much to bear. It may appear that we're standing at the bottom of a long dark staircase leading nowhere, with a climb that seems impossible to trudge. But if we focus on the very first step, the resolve will become clearer.

We must allow the Light of hope to shine on our shoes to give us the courage and determination to take that step. Then we persevere to the next step and the next. Placing one foot carefully in front of the other will make the journey possible.

> . . . we know that suffering produces perseverance; perseverance, character; and character, hope." (Romans 5:4 NIV)

Simply put, we'd like suffering to immediately produce hope, the easy way, but persevering develops character, an individuality that sets us apart. And hope comes with the Light that shines on each step of the staircase of our lives.

Prayer of Perseverance

Almighty God, please give me the will to persevere when it seems I have nothing left to make that step forward. I know that You want to bring light into my darkness. I ask that You illuminate Your light of hope into my circumstances and into my life. In the gracious name of Jesus I pray. Amen.

CHAPTER 7

The Butterfly

September 17, 1999

Now, for everyone can see
I'm a believer in you when you told me,
Told me everything I didn't know,
I'm glad you set me free.
—Sarah Cullison

WHEN I WOKE UP THE MORNING OF FRIDAY, SEPTEMBER 17, I sighed knowing today would be the last day of the three consecutive days we had some sort of ceremony honoring Sarah. The first day, Wednesday, was visitation at the funeral home. The second day was her funeral at our church. This day, the third day, was her burial. This was a private ceremony with family and close friends. It was time to say our final goodbyes.

I can't explain why I thought my emotions would be downhill once this day was over. As a mother saying goodbye to her baby girl, I think I was just hoping it would be.

I sat in the hot sun on a wobbly metal chair perched on a blanket of artificial, worn grass within five feet of the box that held the body of my little girl. I clutched a tissue that would capture my tears as the small group of people watched our pastor bring a short message of hope and heaven.

The casket was a light rose color glistening in the sun. The painted pink roses were appropriately spaced on every handle and a spread of pink and yellow roses, Sarah's favorite color, laid across the top. The roses were wilting after understandably being displayed for several days. I felt my will begin to wilt. I didn't want to do this. I wanted to run away and pretend this never happened. An ache throbbed in the pit of my stomach.

Then, a beautiful monarch butterfly landed on the roses and stayed there gently brushing its wings back and forth for the entire ceremony until we stood to sing a song together. Then it gently flew away, a simple sign of saying goodbye. And a gentle reminder that what was once entombed in a cocoon had now developed into a beautiful new being flying free into the heavens. This beauty represented a message to me that Sarah was safe and finally free in God's presence.

Before anyone approached me, I stood up and made my way to the casket. I needed one more hug. Just one more last hug. I leaned my body over the top end of the casket and tears flowed as I grasped on tightly. I didn't want to let go. I didn't want to say goodbye. I ached, as if someone had thrown a javelin into the center of my heart.

My husband finally pulled me off. I wanted to stay until the very last shovel of dirt covered her grave, but we weren't allowed to. As we drove away, I looked back one more time. I wanted to run back and protect her. I wanted to rescue her from this demise. I wanted to believe it wasn't really true.

This void and loss that I felt segued into a deep longing for heaven. Heaven seemed so close at times, the longing for the arms of Jesus an everyday emotion. I wanted to feel the peace and the freedom that's promised in the forever land. When you lose someone close to you, it's not uncommon to think about heaven and long for heaven.

> But I will sing of your strength, in the morning I will sing of your love; for you are my fortress, my refuge in times of trouble. (Psalm 59:16 NIV)

For the next few months, Ray and I talked a lot about going to the Holy Land. We've always wanted to go in years past, but now the desire was stronger than it had ever been. To us, it was going to God's homeland, a second heaven.

A few months later Ray and I solidified our plans to tour Egypt, Greece, and Israel. In June of 2000 we toured many sites, places where Jesus walked and where Jesus died. As we walked through the garden surrounding Jesus's tomb, I felt at home. It was beautiful in this garden. An array of beautiful trees and flowers surrounded the winding pathways. Sparrows chirping in the trees drowned annoying noises outside the holy walls. It soothed my soul. I took a deep breath and closed my eyes, relishing the moment. As I exhaled, I realized I had not been able to breathe that deeply for months.

As we approached the tomb, a cool breeze brushed my face and lifted my hair, giving my heart a breath of fresh air. I walked through this magnificent garden of beauty and a smile formed on my face. As I stepped into the tomb, conviction pressed me to examine my own sin. I wanted to mourn, but I couldn't. I remembered times following my little girl's death that I couldn't stop crying. Then there were times, for whatever reason, I couldn't cry at all.

I thought to myself, *If I could cry now, surely healing would come.* I reflected on the pain Jesus suffered on the cross for me. Then slowly a tear rolled down my cheek. A spirit of worship grew in my heart, and I felt grateful. After another deep breath, I exhaled, easier still.

Return to your rest, my soul, for the LORD has been good to you. (Psalm 116:7 NIV)

I looked down at the winding path before me. Several white butterflies fluttered around our ankles. Oddly, there were only pure white butterflies, no other color. They seemed playful like giggling children on a playground. It was mesmerizing. They didn't separate, and they didn't change positions; they just floated, suspended there specifically for us.

I said to Ray, "Look at these white butterflies. They are like little angels."

"Look, Sherri," Ray said as he pointed down. "There's a yellow butterfly."

When I saw the yellow butterfly, I gasped. Could this be God telling us Sarah was with Him? After all, a butterfly is the symbol of new life. My suffering soul felt relief as if the Lord's arms had gently wrapped themselves around me and held me close. The darkness in my soul lifted. My empty cup filled with the comfort of God's love. I was safe. I was touched. We knew the Lord was telling us that everything was going to be okay, and that Sarah had found new life with Him. We felt such peace.

Everywhere we walked the yellow butterfly followed us. We couldn't escape. I felt a renewed glimmer of hope that day. It was the most powerful display of God's love yet during this nightmarish journey we were on, obviously a tender message that burst into an epiphany of the divine love of Christ. It was also a very prominent message from God that Sarah was safe in His arms. And so were we.

> I will sing of the Lord's great love forever; with my mouth
> I will make your faithfulness known through all generations.
> (Psalm 89:1 NIV)

The following year Ray was in a season of heavy struggle with Sarah's loss and decided to visit a friend in Idaho. As he drove, it began to rain. The smell of a fresh rainfall permeated inside the car. Ray took a deep breath and enjoyed the natural scent of every plant and bush outside being fed by the rain. He prayed, thanking God for the safe travel and the cool rain. He asked God to give Sarah a hug for him. He looked out the passenger window and there in the sky was a beautiful rainbow, but this wasn't a rainbow like we know them. This rainbow was only one color. *Yellow.*

Ray usually asks God to hug Sarah for him when he finishes his prayers, but this time God hugged Ray. He was given a hug through the subtle expression of a rainbow, the representation of God's promises.

Maybe right now you're not feeling even a glimmer of hope. Maybe you're in the middle of a nightmare situation in your life and you're wondering if God really exists and if He really loves you. You feel like He's abandoned you and you have nothing left to give. Your glimmer of hope has been snuffed out, extinguished completely. Remember this:

> It is the Lord who goes before you. He will be with you; He will not leave you or forsake you. Do not fear or be dismayed." (Deuteronomy 31:8 ESV)

The stories about my grief walk may even cause you to realize that you feel disconnected with God. But I'm here to encourage you that there is no one like Jesus and there's no one that's going to rescue you like He can. You feel you're drowning in an ocean with waves that never return to shore. You're stuck out in the middle in the hot sun, frantically paddling just to stay afloat. Every direction you look there's no shoreline to run to, only water meeting the horizon. You look behind, you look ahead, and there's no promise of freedom from danger or suffering. Remember this:

> This is my command—be strong and courageous! Do not be afraid or discouraged. For the Lord your God is with you wherever you go. (Joshua 1:9 NLT)

Whether you are living in victory or whether you are living in defeat, nothing, and I mean *nothing*, can separate you from His love. Read and believe, dear one. Hold tight to this monumental promise from the very Lord of your soul.

Separation is sometimes temporary and sometimes permanent. I immediately think of a married couple who has separated. There are possibilities of the love story being joined back together or possibly never recovering. No matter the end result, there was separation at some point.

Then there's the mother and baby who were possibly separated at birth. Once the baby grows into an adult, she locates the mother, and they reestablish a relationship. At the beginning of the relationship, there was still separation. Relationships, jobs, homes. We can separate from each one of those, but again, even if we reconcile or even get a new job or a new home, at one time or another we separated from the original one.

Scripture tells us that nothing can separate us from the Lord's love. It sounds like all troubles in life are covered in these verses. Death can't separate us. Life can't. That's a strong promise for a mother like me who once worried that God must not have loved my little girl because He let her die. No, that was a lie I tousled about in my cloudy mind. Not even death can separate us. Not even a suicide death can separate Sarah from His love. Our loved ones who have died are loved by Him. They are precious to Him. Psalm 116:15 (ESV) says, "Precious in the sight of the Lord is the death of his saints."

Our fears, our worries, nothing in all creation can separate you from the love of Christ. The love is unconditional. The love is inseparable. The love is invincible, too powerful to be defeated. That's the level of love no one or nothing can compare to. It's deeper than any ocean and higher than any height. It's stronger than a love between a husband and wife, lifelong friends, or a mother and child. All of these may be separated, but we cannot be separated from the love of Jesus.

I'm sorry if you have been separated from someone you love very much. I'm here to encourage you because I too have felt disconnected, disappointed, unloved, and separated. My purpose is to encourage you that the love like no other has not been severed from your lifeline. I'm throwing you a rope to grab onto so that when you lose your strength, treading in deep waters, you will have a hand to grasp and pull you to safety. It begins with a plea for help. People who are stranded often will send a Morse code message "SOS" to alert others that they're in trouble and need to be rescued. Did you know typically that the abbreviation "SOS" is often referred to as "save our souls?" Yes, Lord, help us . . . save our souls.

As we walk through this journey of grief, help comes in so many ways. Maybe you have to swim yourself all the way to the shore. Remember that you're not alone. Maybe someone reaches out to you and helps you into the boat of rescue. Remember someone sent them.

Connect with someone who has lost a loved one. Remember you're in this together. And keep close contact with those you love.

Please allow me to speak hope over your life. Allow me to reach up to heaven on your behalf. Allow me to send an SOS out for you. I want you to be rescued. I want you to have hope. I want you to believe that God is on your side and that He stands up for you and fights for you. I want you to feel loved. He has not abandoned you or forgotten you. He loves you more than anyone else loves you or ever has. Anyone. Ever.

> Can anything ever separate us from Christ's love? Does it mean He no longer loves us if we have trouble or calamity, or are persecuted, or hungry, or destitute, or in danger, or threatened with death? . . . No, despite all these things, overwhelming victory is ours through Christ, who loved us. And I am convinced that nothing can ever separate us from God's love. Neither death nor life, neither angels nor demons, neither our fears for today nor our worries about tomorrow—not even the powers of hell can separate us from God's love. No power in the sky above or in the earth below—indeed, nothing in all creation will ever be able to separate us from the love of God that is revealed in Christ Jesus our Lord. (Romans 8:35, 37–39 NLT)

Prayer of Hope

Dear Father, You are my Hope. You are the Healer and the Sanctifier of my soul. My hurts and my emptiness can be filled by You, and I believe that. Right now I pray that You will pour into me Your grace and Your favor. Your abundance of life is offered to me freely, and I grasp it with all that I am. I will gladly run with it with You by my side. In the powerful name of Jesus. Amen.

CHAPTER 8

The Gifts

September 14, 1999

Oh death, where is your sting
Oh grave, where is your victory
Cuz we know that Sarah's hope lies in the empty tomb
Of the man from Galilee.
—Christian Joseph

"SHERRI," HANNAH SAID AFFIRMINGLY, "I WANT TO TAKE YOU shopping today to find you a dress for the service." We had temporarily moved in with Bill and Hannah until changes on our house were done.

"Hannah, no, I couldn't have you do that," I humbly replied. After all, they had done so much for us already.

"I insist," she replied.

Later that day, I said goodbye to Ray, and Hannah and I went shopping for a dress.

Oh, how God works. The kindness, the generosity, the overflow from family and friends' hearts flooded us. We were overwhelmed with the love and support from everyone.

Sarah had her freshman year school photo taken four days before she died, and the photography company called me and expressed their condolences and advised me they had been notified that Sarah had died and were sending Sarah's photos by express mail. Oh, my heart. The blessings came from all over the country.

Among more cards and money that came in through the mail, this particular day I received a small box. I didn't recognize the name or the address. Inside was a picture of Jesus in a gold frame with a caption, "Jesus, I trust in you." A note was included that said, "You may not know me, but I heard about your daughter and I felt strongly that I needed to give you this. I hope it brings you comfort." I felt a wave of peace come over me. I stared at the picture, and the anxiety from the world around me settled. The sunken sadness subsided. There was no longer the pain and the sorrow. I felt grateful, and I felt the heart of Jesus. I closed my eyes and smiled. That picture still stands on the bookshelf in my home, a forever keepsake from someone I never knew.

Three days following the phone call from the photography company, a representative from her high school delivered the packet of school pictures that I would normally be excited to see. Oh, yes, I was excited to see them, but then again, I was afraid. I was afraid they wouldn't be good. I was afraid there would be no smile. I was so afraid that my hands shook as I opened the package. I slid the large 8x10 photo out, and it was absolutely beautiful. Sarah's smile was perfect. Her smile beamed with happiness, and her eyes sparkled with life. Her blouse was a soft lavender, a blouse her sister had lent her to wear. The blouse completed the photo. It was perfect.

The last time I saw Sarah's eyes, they were dead. I can't erase that image from my mind. Ever. Yet this blessing of life in her eyes, a smile that displayed happiness, gave me hope. Hope that I didn't fail. She still had life the days before. She still smiled. She still was so beautiful.

My brother David and wife Rebecca had this school picture and her pom picture matted and framed with small gold plates at the bottom with her name and Kingman High School Freshman Pom 1999–2000. Everyone wanted to give to ease our pain. I was moved to tears many times with a grateful heart. I never knew people cared so much for us to send their love in gifts and cards and visits and flowers. I was humbled and so thankful.

The members of our church youth group were hurting. They didn't understand Sarah's death, and their hearts ached too. A group of youth showed up at my parent's home four days after the horrible night. We invited them into the small living room. There were about seven of them. As they came in the door, each one hugged us. Their eyes were sad and some wiped away tears, yet they had come to express their condolences to us.

We all sat down—some of them on the floor as if they were waiting for words, waiting for an explanation, waiting for answers. They nestled in a group as a nest full of young birds, anxiously waiting for their mother to bring them food.

Ray started the conversation. "Thank you all for coming to see us. Losing Sarah has been hard for us, and I also know it's been hard for all of you. I want you to know that what happened to Sarah is not your fault. It was Sarah's unfortunate choice that she made, a very, very wrong choice."

A few of the kids nodded in agreement.

"Don't blame yourselves. Look to God for strength. Keep holding onto your faith no matter what," Ray encouraged.

A few of them hung their heads as if to indicate they were blaming themselves.

"I want you to know that nobody knows why God allowed this to happen, but He did. And it's hard for us to understand, but we have to keep asking Him for strength. I've been struggling, and it's hard, very hard. But then God led me to verses in Isaiah that immediately moved me and comforted me. The verses eased my confusion and my guessing for answers. The Scripture somehow helped me to understand why He allowed Sarah to take her own life," Ray said.

"What we do know is that she is now safe in His presence," he said with conviction.

Then he shared the Scripture.

The righteous man perishes, and no one lays it to heart; and merciful and devout men are taken away, with no one considering that the uncompromisingly upright and godly person is taken away from the calamity and evil to come [even through wickedness]. He [in death] enters into peace; they rest in their beds, each one who walks straight and in his uprightness. (Isaiah 57:1-2 Amp)

"We love you guys, and with the Lord's help, we'll get through this."

The group lingered with us for a bit, chatting with one another mostly. I'm sure they just wanted to encourage us and express their sadness for us too.

The youth leader called me days later and told me that the youth group was going to plant a tree on the church grounds in honor of Sarah. They had a gold plaque made to be nailed to a large rock by the tree. It read:

In Loving Memory of Sarah Renee Cullison
July 8, 1985–September 10, 1999

Then followed by the entire Scripture of Isaiah 57:1–2.

Another friend from church gave me a small bookmark with a poem. It reminded me that God is with me every day and in the days to come. It now sets in the frame of the Jesus picture.

My mother gave me a beautiful music box that played the song *My Heart Will Go On*.

My nephew washed and detailed our car for our drive to the funeral. The number of things people did for us to express their love and concern overwhelmed us.

Our friend Bruce graciously handled all the financial affairs, including the bank account matters, money deposited and dispersed. What a tremendous burden off our shoulders at a time when it was hard to concentrate.

A friend of Ray's invited him to play golf. Some people might not have understood that he went out and enjoyed himself, but it helped to take his mind off his grief just for a little while.

A group of Sarah's friends gathered many photos of their fun times together with Sarah and made a collage and gifted us with it. It hangs in my music room, a gift I'm sure my Sarah would have used since she loved to sing and play piano and her flute. Also, a group of girls from the cheerleading and pom teams from Sarah's school started a Bible study group as a result, and a few girls accepted Christ in their hearts.

A group of close Christian friends offered to come to our home and walk through it and pray over it and bless it. This was when one of them, Debbi, comforted me with a Scripture quote: Lamentations 3:22–23.

> Because of the Lord's great love we are not consumed, for his compassions never fail. They are new every morning; great is your faithfulness. (Lamentations 3:22–23 NIV)

This verse came from friends, from my reading, in sympathy cards, even on the radio. It was coming at me almost daily. It was God.

Then we found a poem Sarah had written titled *Thank You, God*. (The entire poem is located in the back of the book.) What a beautiful gift. It mentions several times how God made her see what she didn't know before. That's eye-opening for me. She knew Him.

Sarah had accepted Jesus into her heart about five years earlier and was baptized by her dad. What a special day that was. This little nine-year-old girl with short brown hair and a white gown over her clothes slowly stepped down into the chilly water of the church baptismal. With a smile on her face, she openly professed her belief that Jesus died on the cross for her sins and that she wanted to live for Him. She believed. It was God's promise to her, and her commitment to Him, that He would always be with her and take her to heaven when her life was through. There is a freedom we feel when we have an eternal hope knowing where we're going at the end of life. Sarah knew that freedom.

Can you say you've experienced that freedom? Or is life weighing you down, and you're sinking? You may feel like you're surrounded by nothing but water and barely keeping afloat. Every time you reach for a preserver, you sink again. Perhaps you feel like your life is falling into a black hole and water is swirling around you, spiraling your life out of control, and it seems there's nothing you can do to save it. Circumstances around you may have become so overwhelming that you can't see the sky above you. You feel helpless and can't catch your breath. You're drowning.

Let me speak over you, my dear friend. Let me throw you a lifeline and pull you to rescue if I may.

There is life.

There is breath.

There is hope.

There is far more for you than you can imagine.

This mess is only temporary. Just as the tide came in, the water will recede. You may see no way out of this wave of despair, but I'm here to tell you that, at this very moment, God predestined you to be reading these words. It takes you and it takes me. Together we can pull each other out of the water. And here's how I know.

> Since God had planned something better for us so that only together with us would they be made perfect. (Hebrews 11:40 NIV)

Just as we set our alarm clock to wake up in the morning, God has set the world in place, and in every second He is involved. He determines our days and everything in them. He predestined this. He predestined our meeting together. Only the King of all creation can orchestrate such a rescue. No coincidence, no oopsies, no happenstance. He is all-knowing and all-powerful. He knows what you need. He knows what you're facing. And just like Paul wrote in Acts 17:26–28 (NIV),

> From one man he (God) made all the nations, that they should inhabit the whole earth; and he marked out their appointed times in history and the boundaries of their lands. God did this so that they would seek him and perhaps reach out for him and find him, though he is not far from any one of us. "For in Him we live and move and have our being."

There is no one like the Lord. God knows every little intricate detail of our lives, and He wants to be right there in the middle of them. Let me encourage you to seek Him, reach out for Him, and you'll find Him. He's not far. He's right here with you and desires you to come to Him.

In the midst of your storm, believe. Take that one small step and reach for the hand that will pull you out of the water into His arms. He'll restore your breath and your strength. He will give you wisdom in choices you may have to make, and He will give you wisdom in restoring what was lost.

> Oh, how great are God's riches and wisdom and knowledge! How impossible it is for us to understand his decisions and his ways! For who can know the Lord's thoughts? Who knows enough to give him advice? (Romans 11:33–34 NLT)

Prayer of Freedom

Lord, I thank You that I am Your craftmanship and that You desire to be close to me. But I also realize that I need to draw close to You. So right now, Father, I reach out my hands with all that weighs them down and reach them toward You. Please touch my hands and pull me to You and into Your arms. Settle my panic, Lord, and give me peace. Breathe into me hope and freedom. Fill me with wisdom from Your heart. My heart is heavy and tired sometimes, but right now I release my heaviness and worry, and believe You for better things. You are my Life Giver and my Gift Giver, and I thank You, Father, for the freedom You give. I pray in the name of the Gift Giver, Jesus. Amen.

CHAPTER 9

The Dance

September 24, 1999

Since You came in my life You changed me all around,
You picked me up when I was down.
—Sarah Cullison

SARAH LOVED TO DANCE. SHE TRIED OUT FOR THE POM-POM line and made it during seventh through ninth grades. I was so proud because my oldest daughter Namantha and myself had been pom-pom dancers as well.

Sarah's pom-pom line sponsor and mother of one of the pom girls, called me and invited us as a family to attend a high school football game on Friday night. She told me that the girls decided as a group to dedicate their halftime performance to Sarah. Oh, my heart. Blessings were still coming from every direction to ease the pain.

We went to the football game and watched parents and students cheer their team on. Ray and I sat there thinking back to when we'd come and watch Sarah perform. It was hard. It was very hard. I expected her to run up with her big smile all dressed in her uniform, ready to make us proud. But she didn't. We saw a few of her friends, and they ran up to hug us. The aching in my stomach was almost too much to bear.

With my stomach flip-flopping, I watched the two-minute warning tick until halftime, and I grabbed Ray's hand and held tight. As halftime arrived, we watched the girls slowly walk out onto the grass field. The announcer was hard to hear because people in the crowd were running to the restroom or the snack stand, but I did hear this:

"The pom line would like to dedicate tonight's performance to Sarah Cullison and her family." My eyes welled up with tears. I had to hold them back from falling down my face. I had to be strong. At least I thought I did.

I expected a lively dance like usual, but the song started slow. The girls in their uniforms moved slow and graceful like a well-rehearsed ballet. This was rare, you know. Normally the music is loud and fast. The girls move fast and jump and often run. I watched in awe; my eyes were glued. The music drew me in. The crowd, the noise, all faded. All I heard was the song *Angel* by Sarah McLachlan being played.

Sarah, their friend and fellow dancer, had become their angel. Gone too soon. Never forgotten. The emptiness that filled their hearts spilled forth as they danced. Their slow movement flowed out of them as healing. The song ended with the girls grouped together leaning on one another's shoulders. This display of affection emitted their current situation, leaning on one another to help endure this time of mourning.

Before we left that night, a few of the girls told us that when they went to pom camp a couple of months before, the teachers taught a routine to this song for anyone who wanted to learn. Some thought they'd never use it, since normally their music was celebratory and upbeat. Some felt compelled to learn it but still were perplexed because they didn't think they would ever perform it. Until now. They performed it for Sarah. They performed it to subside the ache in our hearts. And the ache in theirs.

Four years later, in 2003, Sarah's friends had finished their last year of high school. They learned how to go on. They learned how to smile again, and they learned how to prepare for their future. Four years later I hadn't really learned how to prepare for Sarah's future that no longer existed. I longingly wondered if we should attend her high school graduation. I wondered if it would be too hard for her friends for us to be there when it's supposed to be a fun and exciting night. When we received an invitation in the mail from her high school, thoughts bounced around in my head like a hundred ping-pong balls being hit against a wall.

"Oh how I want to be there."

"But should we *really* go?"

"Will we bring the happiness to a downer?"

"I dread going. What will people think?"

"I want people to know I'm still here, still hurting."

"My stomach hurts thinking about it."

"Maybe as long as Ray and our kids go, it'll help."

"I'm embarrassed."

Above all of these emotions I felt, I wanted to have my daughter's diploma, even though she missed three of her four years of high school. She had missed more games, dances, and classes. I didn't want *her* to miss this. After some discussion, Raymond and Namantha agreed to come.

As we arrived at the high school that night, we watched as families and friends marched in carrying bouquets of flowers and bouquets of blue and gold balloons, celebrating the graduates. The flowers emitted a wonderful fragrance in the air. It reminded me of what I had smelled when sitting in front of Sarah's casket at her funeral. Gradually we pushed our way through the crowd of happy people.

Students stood in groups chattering, helping each other adjust their graduation robes and caps. My longing for Sarah to be there for her graduation engulfed my grief. As we slowly walked by a small group of girls fixing each other's hair, I pictured Sarah standing there with her friends, waving and smiling at us as we walked by.

As I turned my head, a balloon smacked me in the face. My daydreaming abruptly ended. The person holding the balloon bouquet quickly apologized, and I trudged on. The crowds of people we passed were happy for this monumental occasion. As fast as I could, I wanted to be as far away from the laughter and hugs and flowers and balloons. I just wanted to run away through the parking lot, down the street, and keep running. But running away wouldn't leave my pain behind. No matter how far I went or how fast I ran, it would've went with me.

As we walked through the crowd onto the football field to find our seats in the designated bleacher area for parents, I hung my head.

Even though it was seven o'clock at night, I wore my sunglasses to hide my recognizable face and the foreseeable tears that I knew without a doubt would show up. The racing of my heart pounded like Clydesdales racing to the finish line. My head throbbed in pain as it became apparent that I was so tense it gave me a headache.

We finally found seats on the second row of the bleachers to fit the four of us, plus a friend of Namantha's who had come with her for support. We squeezed in and sat uncomfortably shoulder to shoulder and watched the crowd of people pile into the stands with their balloons and horns. This wasn't a party for us. This was a substitute for happiness.

"Maybe we shouldn't have come," I said to myself.

"Maybe we should leave."

"I don't think I can do this."

Just then the high school band started to play the well-known anthem for graduations, "Pomp and Circumstance." In the distance, I saw a cluster of royal blue caps and gowns. Slowly, the graduates marched through the parking lot and onto the football field to take their seats for the ceremony.

Sarah would be walking with them if it weren't for...

Looking through the crowd of happy and hollering students, I looked for her. She wasn't there. The ache became more prevalent.

The valedictorian gave her speech and talked of what the future held for the graduates and how to make the best of it. I thought about my own future. There wouldn't be a college to search for with Sarah. There wouldn't be a wedding to plan one day for Sarah. There wouldn't be children or grandchildren of her own. An empty seat at the dining room table was my future. An empty seat in the car. The empty place in my heart sank even further. I tried to close the door on my thoughts, but there was no use. A few hundred high school seniors sat in front of me, excited for their new lives, but I didn't feel excited for mine. There would be no future for Sarah. Her new future was now in the past.

When will this be over? Please hurry. I panicked in my mind.

Finally, the school principal announced she would be presenting diplomas of those students that have passed away to the parents or family members who were present. I felt like I was going to collapse. *I don't want to do this. I can't do this.*

We'll just walk up there real fast, respectfully shake the principal's hand, and quickly walk back to our seats. The very few who remembered her from the first week of her first year of high school nearly four years ago would politely clap and then it will be over.

I thought I had it all figured out. But no, I thought I had to pretend to be proud. I had to envision myself putting one foot in front of the other in heels through thick grass without falling. I had to get through this for my baby girl.

"Lord, please help me," I pleaded under my breath.

Ray fidgeted with his hands, obviously uncomfortable. I slid my hand into his and we gripped each other's hands as tightly as we could. We were both leaning on each other in a physical way, acknowledging this was such a hard thing for us to do. I was so thankful I had him there in that moment.

Finally, the principal announced, "Sarah Renee Cullison." My husband grasped my hand, and we walked together toward the podium for what seemed like twenty miles long. Some of the audience graciously clapped. More joined in. The applause grew louder. And unexpectedly, one by one, the graduating student body stood and clapped. And clapped. And clapped. I realized then that they stood to remember Sarah and to acknowledge our pain. In the midst of my fogged mind, as we were accepting Sarah's diploma from the school principal, I heard shouts from her classmates, her friends. They were encouraging us without a single word, reminding us they care.

I thought they had forgotten her. I thought they had moved on into their near-adult lives with Sarah only in their past. But they proved to us just then that she was still in their present. At my husband's leading, we turned and addressed her class. Ray waved, thanking them. I followed suit. How touching. How powerful. How wonderful they were, and they didn't even know they had just given us a hug without even coming close.

As we sat and waited for the rest of the class to be presented with their diplomas, my tied-up emotions continued to unleash through a fountain of tears. One after another, silent tears flowed down my cheeks. They just kept coming and coming. I couldn't wipe them away fast enough. I tried to hide it from the people sitting around us. I don't know why. Surely, they knew we were in pain. All the dread, all the anticipation, all the anxiety flooded the already soaked tissues in my hand.

We couldn't walk out in the middle of the ceremony as much as I wanted to. We needed to show her classmates respect and stay until the end. It was hard for my husband and children too. I saw the sadness on their faces and the tears in their eyes. They were now four years older and had moved on into adulthood. Their lives were drastically different now. Raymond was working a full-time job in adolescent caregiving and living in his own home. Namantha was now married and working as an escrow assistant.

This graduation was one of the hardest events I've experienced. By this time in 2003, we had attended weddings, funerals, and birthday parties, each with their own struggles and sadness, but Sarah's high school graduation impacted me heavily. I can't explain why. Maybe because it's one of life's accomplishments she didn't get to experience. Maybe because for four years I had only seen a few of her friends sporadically, and once now, when her whole class was together for the last time, that's why.

All we could do was hug our kids at that point. A few of Sarah's friends also came over to us and hugged us. No words, really. Just a hug of comfort.

From the moment Sarah lost her life, I've had a lot of hugs. Hugs from family. Hugs from friends. Hugs even from strangers. But the applause and standing ovation was so poignant that I felt as if they had lifted me out of a canyon into a helicopter and onto a gurney after a gruesome crash. This event might have been one of the very hardest, but it was one of those occasions where a hug from many at once was the most prominent.

What is in a hug anyway? An act where two or more people put their arms around each other and hold each other closely, typically expressing affection. A hug usually emits emotional warmth and sometimes arises from joy or happy occasions. Hugs are usually given at happy affairs like weddings, graduations, birthdays, and long-awaited reunions. A hug is a form of endearment to communicate support and love, especially where words are insufficient.

A hug can also make us cry because a hug tells us that we're not alone. When someone hugs us, it helps us to feel safe to express our true feelings and helps us to feel understood in a way that not a single word could represent. Hugging someone who is grieving a loss is a method in which we show compassion and reassurance that everything will be all right.

If you've experienced a loss of someone you love, you know how meaningful a hug is. And if you've felt lost and alone, you also know how meaningful a hug is. A hug is therapy. When all words have been said to someone grieving and you don't know what else to do for them besides pray for them, reach out and give them a hug. No words need to be exchanged. A hug communicates how you care about that person without needing to say a word.

Sometimes we give hugs to say hello and sometimes to say goodbye. Being hugged can also make us feel safe at a time when we feel in danger. Hugs are most often welcomed and can be very important in healing.

Hugging increases our ability to control our feelings, and hugging someone you love for twenty seconds a day is the key to alleviating stress and beating burnout. A lingering embrace releases the hormone oxytocin that scientists sometimes call the "cuddle hormone." It can slow your heart rate, lower your blood pressure, and yes, improve your mood.

I find it comforting when Ray and I pray together, and in those times when he's feeling the loss of Sarah's presence, he ends his prayer asking God to hug Sarah for him. That touches my heart and comforts me too. In that instant, the prayer becomes a hug for me as well. Receiving a hug in a prayer reminds me that one day I'll hold Sarah in my arms. But for now, it's a hug that gives me joy for today.

What do you do when you miss someone you've lost? Do you talk to them? Maybe even hug their pillow?

> Very truly I tell you, you will weep and mourn while the world rejoices. You will grieve, but your grief will turn to joy. (John 16:20 NIV)

Prayer of Joy

Father, sometimes all I see is my little grief-stricken world. Help me to remember the times others have hugged me and made me feel better. Help me to see the grief and needs of others so that I can fill their need with a hug. I'm thankful my tears are stored and that they are counted by You because You care. And thank You for the promise that my grief turns to joy. But for now, hold me tight, Lord. I find comfort there. In the name of my Provider of joy, Jesus. Amen.

CHAPTER 10

The Angel

September 25, 1999

And though we long to see her smiling face
We know that she is safe in Jesus's arms.
—*Christian Joseph*

"COME ON, SHERRI. WE NEED TO GET OUT," RAY INSISTED. "We should be there for the car wash. They're doing this for us."

Two weeks after Sarah's funeral, we were told a group of people from the church were holding a car wash to help with our expenses.

My immediate thought was, *Ugh, do we have to be around people?* I just wanted to stay home in my confined comfortable space. Then I realized that yes, it would be rude not to show up. He was right.

"Do we have to stay long?" I asked.

"Just for a little bit," Ray assured me.

All my life I was uncomfortable around a lot of people, especially people I didn't know. When I was cast into the center of attention, my heart raced. I felt like I had been thrown into a furnace, which made my face flush, and then I was self-conscious about that on top of everything else. Embarrassment would cover me like a blanket, and the room would start to spin, and I would feel confused and full of panic.

For this day, I felt embarrassed. Ashamed. I wondered what people thought of me. Surely, they were thinking I was a terrible mother because my daughter wanted to end her life.

We pulled into the parking lot of a shopping plaza where the car wash was going on. So many of our church friends were there in the scorching heat sweating and obviously tired. A few cars were lined up getting their cars washed. Just as quickly as one got done, another one rolled in. There was a never-ending flow of carwash traffic.

Ray immediately walked over to greet our friends and thank them. He is the social butterfly of our family. I forced myself out of the car and stood on a curb under a tree, making it appear that I needed shade out of the heat.

One by one, I saw several cars drive through, many of whom were good friends that came to support us. I wanted to reach out and thank and hug everyone, but I couldn't. My shame and embarrassment held me back like an invisible wall between us that I couldn't climb or walk through. I was alone, just where I wanted to be.

Just then I heard a woman's voice behind me that in fact startled me. I jolted and turned. There stood a small older woman I had never seen before.

She kept her eyes covered behind her sunglasses and reached out her hand to me. "I don't know who this is for or what this is all about. I don't want my car washed. I just know that I need to help and give this to you," she said hurriedly, slipping something into my hand.

I looked down at a neatly folded twenty-dollar bill. "Thank you," I said, lifting my head to acknowledge her unselfish gift.

But she was gone. I looked to each side and behind me. I stepped off the curb onto the asphalt and turned my whole body in a 360-degree spin, looking for this generous soul to thank her, and I saw nothing. No other person was near me. No other car was near me. Just as quickly as she appeared and startled me, she disappeared.

Perplexed and confused, I walked my way over to the car wash workers. A lady in our church was leading this massive entourage of cars. The flow of traffic never slowed. The workers, some from Sarah's youth group, were sunburned and tired. I wanted to help but knew it wasn't my place. Not now. Ray was still thanking the workers and visiting with the people coming through the line in their cars.

I walked through the cool water and soap on the asphalt that felt refreshing since it was so hot. I maneuvered myself over to my friend, and she warmly smiled and quickly hugged me, excusing herself from sweating and not being able to stop and talk. I thanked her and walked over to where Ray was. I told him what had happened and that I didn't know who the lady was or where she went. I told him how my eyes had scanned the entire block of the parking lot and couldn't find her.

The giver that day was our angel. I truly believe that. It happened too fast. Now I know why I needed to stand under the tree that day by myself. It was so that God could send me an angel. In that moment the rip in my heart mended part way. Thankful tears flowed. I was humbled that God chose me in that vulnerable moment to bless me with a fleeting angel.

There were many angels that day, my friend and her crew, and many friends and people who didn't even know us but who drove through and donated. I didn't want to leave. I wanted to stay and be a part of something that I couldn't believe was happening.

Then I heard a loud diesel engine pull in behind me. I turned around, and there was a big red fire engine idling with two firemen inside. Since Ray had been a volunteer fireman for several years, he immediately walked over to talk to them. The passenger handed Ray something, and I thought, *Did they? Did they really?*

As they drove away, they waved and I waved back. Heart to heart, man to man never felt so warm and humbling. Ray explained that they obviously didn't want to get the fire truck washed, but they had collected cash from other firefighters and gave a generous donation. More angels.

A short while later, gray clouds rolled overhead—a nice cool refresher for the crew. They quickly grabbed a drink from their bottled water and went back to washing and rinsing. Then I felt a drop on my arm. Then one on my face. It was starting to sprinkle. *Surely the car wash would have to stop if it started to rain,* I thought.

Then came another drop and another drop, and within minutes, it was much more than a sprinkle. There were still cars in line that didn't budge, so the crew kept on washing. Just as quickly as they washed the car and started spraying with a hose to rinse, the rain was rinsing the cars clean. A pure water rinse from heaven. The rain fell harder, and cars kept coming. People were paying to have their cars washed in the rain. I felt overcome with thankfulness, overwhelmed with emotion, and touched by angels from a God who still loved me.

I believe we witnessed a miracle that day. In our small town, this five-hour car wash profited nearly $2,500. Can you really say that was a coincidence? No.

I truly believe God sends angels to our rescue for many reasons. Experiencing trauma can be one of those reasons. We don't even realize we suffer from this trauma until something triggers it. Often, it's the way we respond to loud noises and images that remind us of the traumatic experience.

Not long after Sarah died, while watching a movie, I heard gunshots in the movie. I was unnerved. I had that urge again to run away. Even if I paused the movie, I couldn't watch it. Even though I wasn't in the room when Sarah took her own life, the sound of a gunshot reminded me. When I saw blood, I thought of her. When I saw pictures of her, even though she was my little girl and I loved looking at her still full of life, I also saw death. Often times when I walked into her bedroom, I didn't remember her lying on her bed but rather lying on the living room floor.

The most impactful trauma experience for me was when I heard a baby cry. I felt agony.

Within a few weeks after Sarah's death, I was strolling through the grocery store simply shopping for food. Markets can be noisy with baskets rolling around, grocery items being scanned by the checkout clerks, and people talking.

I was having a decent emotional day until I heard a young family on the aisle next to me. A young mother was having trouble keeping her small children corralled long enough to do her shopping. And then it happened. A small child started crying, not whimpering but full-on crying.

I stopped my basket. I felt my hands grip the basket handle tighter. My head started sweating. A gut-wrenching pain invaded my stomach. I looked down at my grocery cart and devised an immediate plan to grab my purse, abandon my basketful of items, and run for the car. The unexplainable ache in my heart was unbearable. I had to run. I had to get away from the painful cries. Hurriedly, I pushed my cart farther down about three aisles. I closed my eyes, took a deep breath, and began to feel a small amount of relief.

The only way I can explain why I felt the way I did was because of the trauma I had experienced. Babies cry and for good reason, but I sincerely believe it was a physiological connection with my baby that I could no longer have. Sarah may have sat there on the floor that night trying to talk herself out of the act, and maybe she had cried. That I'll never know. All I know is maybe the pain in my own heart permeated when I heard the cries of a baby I'll never hold again.

We like to think of babies in heaven as our angels, the ones we treasure and hold close to our hearts. Some mothers never even get to see or hold their babies before they go to heaven, and perhaps God is saving a special place for those mothers and babies to reunite. I sure hope so.

I can't say whether or not Sarah is now an angel, but what I do know is that God has sent me angels when I needed them most. Angels come our way sometimes in the midst of a defining moment of traumatic reminders like I had in the grocery store.

By the time I had reached the checkout counter at the store that day, I felt someone come up behind me and give me a big tight hug. It startled me somewhat, and I turned to see a familiar friend with a beaming smile. She helped me to forget. She was my angel that day.

Maybe you feel like you haven't experienced an angel blessing, but I encourage you to believe and to be watchful. It might be a phone call from a friend with words of encouragement. Maybe it's a card in the mail or hearing a song on the radio. Maybe it's a much-needed hug from someone you love. Whatever it may be, angels come to help us heal.

> In my desperation I prayed, and the LORD listened; he saved me from all my troubles. For the angel of the LORD is a guard; he surrounds and defends all who fear him. (Psalm 34:6–7 NLT)

Most prominently angels are thought of a lot around Christmastime. There are several Christmas carols about angels. Many decorations around the holiday include angels. Somehow, the presence of a representation of angels give us solace, a peace, or a calm. We think of them as heavenly beings or celestial creatures. But they are enigmatic, a curiosity at best. Unfortunately, I don't have the complete understanding of angels, but I do know God uses them to minister to us.

So often I was asked the question how others can help when we're walking through the storms of grief. When I pick up our mail from the mailbox, most of the time there are bills to be paid or what we call junk mail, items we toss in the trash. But when I see an envelope addressed from a personal friend, I'm rather curious to open it. So many times I've received cards in the mail that are so uplifting. Immediately my spirit is encouraged. These days messages in social media or an email are the way most people communicate with each other, but there is nothing more personal than receiving a card in the mail. It lets us know that someone is thinking about us, that we haven't been forgotten, and that Sarah hasn't been forgotten.

Another way to be an angel to someone hurting is to simply call them on the phone. Sure, we don't know exactly what to say, but all we need to say is that we're thinking about them and are there for them. We may hesitate to say if there's anything we can do, please let us know, but for a person grieving a loss, it's best to do something for them. The majority of the time, the person is not going to call you back and let you know what they need. Take that initiative to help. Be an angel to the rescue for them. Friends periodically called Ray and I just to genuinely ask how we were getting along. You can almost predict the answer to that question, but at least you're showing that you're concerned and that you care.

As the Word tells us, we are to entertain strangers. Okay, I hear you. Strangers? We like our cliques, don't we? We like our family and familiar friends. We're comfortable with them. Let me tell you about a stranger who became an angel for me.

At the end of Sarah's funeral service, Ray, the kids, and I went over to the fellowship hall of our church where we had a reception line so those attending could greet us and give their condolences. We hugged family. We hugged friends. We cried with many who came hundreds of miles just to be there for us that day. Many people I hadn't seen for years. And then as a woman made her way toward me, I was thinking I had seen her before and even knew her name as Debbie, but I had never met her. She approached me and took my hand in hers.

"Sherri, you don't know me, but I want you to know that I have gone through what you're going through right now. I lost my little girl too," she said confidently. She then handed me a gift bag.

"Here is a book that someone gave me when I was grieving, and it helped me. It helped me a lot. And I'm sure it'll help you as you grieve for Sarah," she said with a smile.

I thanked her, she quickly hugged me, and then she was gone. The next person in line was hugging me before I realized I should have thanked the woman better. But she was my angel that dreadful day. She could've never come. She could've never brought the book. She could've never been there for me that day. She didn't know me just as I didn't know her. She ministered to me even though we were strangers. Thankfully, I've gotten to know her better over the years, and many times I've run into her now and then around town and I'm reminded of my angel moment.

> Do not forget to show hospitality to strangers, for by so doing some people have shown hospitality to angels without knowing it. (Hebrews 13:2 NIV)

Prayer of Help
God in heaven, I thank You that You send angels to me to diminish my trauma and to remind me of Your goodness. Help me to be attentive to those tender moments when someone extends kindness. And help me to be an angel to someone else who desperately needs a moment of help. In the name of my Helper, Jesus. Amen.

CHAPTER 11

The Necklace

September 26, 1999

How great it is to have You in my life, and You will not leave
'Cause my dream, You brought it true. God, I love You.
—*Sarah Cullison*

AS I LOOKED IN THE DRESSER MIRROR TO CHECK MY HAIR one more time before leaving for church, I analyzed the older me. More wrinkles, more puffiness around the eyes, less smile lines. These last three weeks since we lost Sarah had worn on my face. I shrugged the disappointment away, accepting that I couldn't do anything about it.

The bedroom door opened, and Ray walked in holding a cup of coffee. "I had a dream about Sarah last night."

"Did you?"

Ray had been longing to dream about Sarah for a couple of weeks since we lost her. I had dreamed of her, her friends had, and other family members had, but it frustrated Ray that he didn't have a dream with her in it. When you've lost someone close, it's gratifying to see them alive, to feel their presence, even if it's in a dream. Ray described the dream to me.

"I was sitting in the living room and in walked Sarah and a friend. Sarah had a smile on her face, and she moved and talked as if she were there in the room. I kept telling her that I loved her, and she just smiled and said, 'I know, Dad.'

"She asked me where you were, and I told you were in the kitchen, so she and her friend walked into the kitchen. As you were washing the dishes, she handed you a gift, a necklace, and then left.

Disappeared. Just like that. I just kept telling her over and over that I loved her. I just wanted her to know that I loved her. The dream was so real."

Have you ever had a dream like that? Sleep is a curious mystery to me. We fall into a state of lull in our minds and bodies. And it's as though time stops with us but not for the rest of the world. The clock keeps ticking, people keep going about, and the world keeps moving. But not us. As we sleep, there seems to be a void where we don't remember sometimes hours that were ahead of us and are now behind us.

Some of us make a habit of praying before we fall asleep. Still some of us may read or even watch television. Often, we may not even have the Lord on our minds as we're drifting off into dreamland. What's your routine? Are you guilty, like me, of falling asleep with only the thought that you're so sleepy and you can't keep your eyes open anymore? Do you know that God is with you? Do you realize that He's right there in the room with you? The Word reminds us that He watches over us even as we sleep.

> In peace I will lie down and sleep, for you alone, O LORD, will keep me safe. (Psalm 4:8 NLT)

After losing someone you love, unexplained fear and anxiety accompany you. Fear that you'll lose someone else close to you, fear of the darkness at night, fear that's incomprehensible. It can overtake our minds and cause us to have difficulty breathing, anticipating something bad is going to happen. These emotions can envelop you, making it hard to sleep. Our mind becomes a racetrack with each race car acting as another item of worry. Without realizing it, the whizzing of the cars in our minds continues as we lie down to sleep. My mind won't stop sometimes. I feel my heart racing with every turn of every thought. Sometimes I feel as though it won't ever stop.

Pray. Ask the Lord for the peace that passes all understanding. Take a deep breath and exhale slowly, releasing every care and worry, and trust Him. Why? Because this:

Then Jacob awoke from his sleep and said, "Surely the LORD is in this place, and I wasn't even aware of it!" (Genesis 28:16 NLT)

We forget, don't we? We forget the Holy Spirit is always there to comfort us, to drop our cares to, and to allow Him to quietly help us drift off into a dream of peaceful sleep.

Some experts recommend a glass of warm milk before bedtime. Hmm, not sure I like that idea, but maybe some of you do. Maybe add a little chocolate, and I'll call it good. How about you? Some experts recommend a cup of hot tea or maybe even an essential oil may help. I'm okay with all of that, but cuddling up in a big blanket and rolling myself into a little ball as if I'm in the safe place of my mother's womb is calming to me. Closing my eyes and imagining the Lord kneeling gently beside my bed gives me comfort. I like the word *comfort*. Com-fort. It's almost a plea for a fort to come to us, surround us, and keep us safe.

I *loved* building forts with my siblings when we were growing up. We'd gather big empty boxes and put them with blankets and pillows, sometimes draping sheets over the top. It was a cozy space that emitted a feeling of warmth and relaxation. Even though the walls of the fort, or rather the walls of the empty boxes, were thin and flimsy, to us it was strong and elusive. We pretended we were guards of the fort and although others tried to work their way in, we held our ground guarding the so-called gates. We felt invincible like superheroes. Somehow, we gained this assurance in our imaginative minds that we could stop anything that got in our way. We eluded fear and worry. We had built a fort that surrounded us beyond all odds.

Com-fort. A calm that releases our fears and brings courage. Tonight, as you lie in bed and are trying to fall asleep and can't, say a prayer asking for com-fort. Maybe it'll take you back to a happy time when you built a fort as a child and will help you fall asleep with a smile on your face. I really hope so. I hope you find rest tonight and have pleasant dreams. You are safe. You are loved. You are wrapped in com-fort.

Later, on the morning Ray told me about his dream with Sarah bringing me a gift, we went to church. It was a typical Sunday morning until the pastor, without any tip-off, announced that a group of ladies would be presenting a special gift to our daughter Namantha and myself. As a special token of their love in a time of loss, the ladies bought a necklace for each of us. The necklace was silver in the shape of a teardrop and inside the teardrop was etched the design of a rose. Included in the box was the written explanation of how the necklace was designed. A woman jeweler had recently lost a close family member and was mourning that loss. As she sat at her desk on a phone call, she sketched the initial design of the rose.

The beauty of a rose is unique. Its petals are soft like velvet and emit an aroma unlike other flowers. Perhaps the sketch was a reminder that there was beauty even in her tears. Gradually it developed into the necklace and included in the box were the reassuring words that God is always with us.

We both felt very humbled and appreciative of this special gift, but the ladies had no idea how God had worked in and through this whole situation. I was astounded. Did this really just happen? A dream really came true. Sarah brought a gift in the dream to Ray the night before, and that gift fell into my hands the next morning.

When Ray's eyes met mine after the presentation that Sunday morning, we both knew how God had given him a gift with a dream of Sarah and how he was able to tell her many times how he loved her. And then I received a gift of the necklace, and this wasn't the only gift God had given me that day. We were given the gift of hope. There was no doubt in our minds that this was the result of a gift-giving God who touched our hearts that day. His voice boomed in our lives that Sunday morning. There was no mistaking that He wanted us to know in so many ways that He was there with us, and that we were safe and loved.

Every good and perfect gift is from above, coming down from the Father of the heavenly lights, who does not change like shifting shadows. (James 1:17 NIV)

Maybe you haven't experienced a gift like this. Maybe your circumstances are such that the road ahead looks bleak and hopeless. Look along your path, my friend. The Lord will bring people into your lives, whether it be a dream or in real life, who are there for a purpose.

If you're struggling in your circumstance, find someone you trust and tell them. Tell them your need. Maybe it's just a hug. Maybe it's financial help you need. Maybe it's a friend who can help you build a fort that'll help strengthen you and give you hope. We need each other in a world that seems so cruel sometimes. God will bring others into your life to encourage you and counsel you.

Maybe you know someone who is going through an especially hard life matter, and you feel as though there's nothing you can do to help them. You might not be able to help them get out of tremendous debt. But be their lifeboat. Just be there for them. Call them and offer to give them a ride to church each week to defray expenses. Or take the abused wife house hunting. Or watch the newspaper for a possible job for an unemployed husband of your friend. There are so many simple ways to help if we just set aside ourselves and allow God to work through us. Pray that God will reveal to you how you can help.

Often people in trouble just need a real friend—someone to talk to, to spend time with, and to encourage them that everything will be okay. When we feel lost and abandoned in our circumstances, all we need sometimes is someone who will come alongside of us and take us by the hand to a place where we can forget about the deep well we feel we've fallen into even if just for a moment.

Wells are dark and cold and wet. We don't know what type of mental demons we may wrestle with in this hole, and many times we're not ready to even recognize them until they have a stronghold on us. One of those strongholds can be depression. We can allow ourselves to relax into a belief that nothing is going to change until all we want to do is get lifted out of the muck and be lifted to safety to the warm sunshine at the top.

Depression includes the suppression of all happiness. It lies to you that you're worthless and that you don't need anyone else to help you. You may have suffered from severe oppression by someone else, and you feel you'd be better off dead. Please don't believe that lie.

Be determined to overcome depression and keep your eyes focused on the light at the top of the well. Reach and strive for the beauty above. If you feel no one knows how you feel, call them out. If one step forward to reach out your hand is all it takes, you're very well worth it. You are a living, breathing being who can have a great relationship with others. The reward is great as life is an indescribable gift.

Over the years friends may come and go in your life, but friends who stay and are there for you in difficult times and who pray for and with you are gifts incarnate. People have asked me how they can be a help to someone suffering, and my first answer is to pray for them and pray with them. Encourage them with a phone call, a note of kindness in the mail, or a simple text saying, "I'm thinking of you."

Once Sarah's services were over, everyone went back to their normal lives, but we didn't. We still grieved for a very long time. We did have wonderful friends and family who came to us in the next few weeks and asked to take us to lunch, sent a card in the mail, or simply gave us a hug as we passed in the grocery store. There is a lot of truth in the fact that little things mean a lot. What might have appeared to have been a small gift to most, the rose-engraved necklace was a monumental gift that lifted us from moments of despair to moments of hope.

> A gift opens the way for the giver and ushers the giver into
> the presence of the great. (Proverbs 18:16 NIV)

Prayer of Comfort

Lord, You are so great and so deserving of my praise. You bring so many gifts in those times I may only think of the special gift I lost. Remind me, Father, of those who are depressed and need a special gift today. The verse above promises not only a gift for the one receiving it, but also a gift for the giver. How wonderful are Your ways. And how wonderful is Your heart that gives the most. In the name of my Comforter, Jesus. Amen.

CHAPTER 12

The Understanding

October 10, 1999

So we won't cry for Sarah, though we miss our Sarah
No sad goodbyes for Sarah, no, we won't cry for Sarah
Because we'll be home to see her soon.
—Christian Joseph

ONE MONTH AFTER LOSING SARAH, WE WERE STILL STAYING with friends Bill and Hannah. I went outside by myself this particular night and stood in the dark. The trees and bushes waved back and forth from the wind. The shadows expelled an eeriness, a mysterious spirit that frightened me. I felt as if I was completely abandoned and alone. Although I stood solid with my feet on the ground, my legs were shaky and weak. A nervous energy in my stomach practically begged me to release it.

I looked up at the sky and there within the black night sky were thousands of stars twinkling as if there was not a care in the world just then. The beauty of their light radiated and lifted my burden for a moment.

"I hope you're happy, Sarah. I miss you. I know you're in heaven. I know you're safe and not miserable anymore, but I don't want to deal with this anymore," I whispered.

"I really hope you're happy," I genuinely said.

"I hope you're happy," I said as my voice grew louder and my brow tightened.

"I hope you're happy," I thrust toward the sky with a loud voice.

The genuine wish for her happiness in a moment turned into aggravated anger. I couldn't believe what I heard in my voice. The shadows faded, I ignored the wind in the trees, my knees were stronger, and I breathed with teeth gritted together in anger. In that moment I gasped.

What am I doing? I thought, perplexed.

How could I be angry at my little girl who I loved more than life itself, now that her life was gone?

I felt ashamed and damaged.

"Please, God, help me. Help me to understand. Help me to understand why. Help me to understand why this happened."

A tear slipped out of my eye, grazed my cheek, and fell to the ground. As I stared at the wet spot on the cement driveway, I examined my reaction when I talked to Sarah in the sky. With each sentence where I stated I hoped she was happy, I had grown angry with her, and I didn't even realize I was angry before this. I analyzed it in my mind over and over again, but I couldn't manage to reach a conclusion. Therefore, my frustration fermented deep down until I became impatient. The impatience then matured into anger.

Have you ever stood at a kitchen counter stirring cake mix ingredients in a bowl by hand? It's a long, slow process. The box told me to pour in the cake mix, then add oil, eggs, and water. Then stir to moisten the mixture. *Then* continue mixing for two full minutes. Two minutes? Two minutes. Yikes. Two minutes is a very long time when you're counting second after second. Okay, so I stirred the mixture and stirred and stirred some more until my arm got tired. So then, I switched arms, and the other arm got tired. I looked up at the clock, and only one minute had passed.

You've got to be kidding me. It's only been a minute. Ugh.

If we allow frustration to build up within us day after day, it can advance into anger and then unleash itself at a time when it might not be wise to.

Standing outside in the dark, talking to Sarah that night, I was frustrated because I couldn't understand why. I got impatient because

I didn't have the answers, and I was not even sure that I would ever have the answers.

The wind picked back up again and rustled a few dead tree leaves around my feet. I cuddled my jacket up closer around me to warm the cold chill. I took a deep breath and exhaled. It was time to go back inside. There was no booming voice announcing answers. No miraculous billboard sign appeared before me. My chest felt heavy again. I couldn't escape it.

How can we understand the ways of mystery? How can we learn the answers to the whys simply by asking? We can look for clues, I suppose, but with no tangible evidence available, how can I ever expect an answer to the biggest question, Why? I can speculate. I can guess. I can even ask others. But do they have the answer? No.

In the days preceding Sarah's death, our church board was in the middle of the process to hire me on staff as worship leader and music director. I had served in this capacity informally for two years, and it appeared it would be a simple process. However, surprisingly, the process was taking much longer than seemed necessary. I was interviewed and requested to give my testimony before the church congregation two days before Sarah died.

The enemy did not want the church to hire me. He was envious and jealous. He is the perpetrator of the worst evil and biggest convincer of no self-worth. He must have thought that he was going to show me who was boss by invading Sarah's thoughts with lies. He thought he would stop this monumental step in my life by ending hers.

Forty-eight hours later, I stood over the body of my dead teenager with a gun in her hand and no life in her body. Satan thought he had won. I thought he had too.

I continued to question again. Why would this happen? Why the darkness would loom over me for weeks when I thought I was going to be happy as the new worship leader of our church. Now I had to plan the funeral for my daughter inside these church walls where I had worshiped God for so long. It wasn't fair. I had been good. She had been good. She had asked Jesus into her heart five years earlier and had been baptized by her dad. She attended youth group, and we even went to youth camp together.

My heart raced more than ever before; my lungs felt like they weren't functioning half the time. Fear overwhelmed me most of the time. Fear I would lose another child. Fear I would lose my husband. Fear and darkness. Darkness and fear. I dreaded the sunsets because that meant the darkness came and darkness meant anxiety—overwhelming, frightening nights where I closed my eyes and saw my daughter lying in a pool of blood. I couldn't believe it had happened to me.

We were a family that did fun things together. Vacations, snow sledding, playing football in the living room, friends and cousins spending the night and building forts, a bowl of ice cream for way too many nights. Times were sometimes hard, but I never knew how hard they were for Sarah. She never revealed she was depressed or sad. She kept her feelings trapped inside of her, and it grew into a destructive weapon.

I admit I had been depressed in my life many times. I felt I had no purpose for my life really, even to become a worship leader. The evil-doer had convinced me with attacks in my own thoughts that I wasn't good at anything. He led me to believe the lies that I was worthless, just like he convinced Sarah she wasn't good enough either.

As my life was slipping away, I remember the LORD. (Jonah 2:7a NLT)

As I grew closer to God in reading His Word and listening to His voice, I discovered a newfound hope for my life. He loves me. He values me. He gifts me. He delights in me. I discovered a new me by discovering Him. I am worth it. I am enough.

As I learned more about God, I learned to understand more than I ever had before. The more I studied, the more I was enlightened. And the more He revealed Himself to me, the more of Him I wanted. I leaned on Him more in the first year of Sarah's death than ever before. Joy and life jumped off my Bible pages at me, and I felt relief. I felt loved. My prayers of graveling for help turned into prayers of thankfulness and confident trust.

You see, God allows us to make choices of whether to succumb to evil or turn to the Light, Himself. God knew beforehand the choice Sarah would make. Could he have stopped it? Yes. Could I have stopped it? Maybe. Maybe not. She could have very well taken her life a week later or even years later. There's no way of knowing. But what I do know is that I can continue spending hours and days and weeks and years trying to figure it all out, but I never will. It belongs in the memory of the distant unknown. I believe the day the Lord takes me home to heaven, He may reveal to me the why, but I'll run into Sarah's arms and it won't matter anymore.

My understanding of Sarah's death is this. The Lord allowed it to happen, even though Satan meant the murder of herself to destroy not only Sarah, but also our family, her friends, and anyone else it might have affected. What the enemy didn't understand at the time is that God took this devastating tragedy and saved lives. Who did He save? He saved me. He saved many family and friends. And He saved you. I'm certain of it. You have been chosen for this very moment in time to read these words to save you. You may be drowning in despair like I was. You may have been given this book as a gift and God foreknew your need. There are no coincidences, my friend. He is perfect. And that's all we need to understand.

As for God, his way is perfect: The LORD's word is flawless." (Psalm 18:30a NIV)

So many circumstances happen because of choices we make. Some good, some bad. I can wonder and guess all day long for the rest of my life why Sarah chose this ending, but the one thing I know is not to lean on my own understanding. Answers I've searched for will be given in God's time, not my own. And still, those answers may never be given in this lifetime. But now, I'm okay with that.

The closer I get to God and the more I learn of His ways, I'm learning to understand *Him*. Believe me, I'll never completely comprehend everything about God, but by learning to understand Him I'm learning to lean on Him more. I'm learning to believe Him more. And I'm learning to love Him more. Proverbs 3:5 (NIV) reads, "Trust in the Lord with all your heart and lean not on your own understanding."

My own understanding was full of confusion and questions. Like a tornado, my mind spun uncontrollably trying to find the answers. A tornado picks up things, spins them around, destroys them, and spits the remnants back to the ground. If we allow it, our thoughts can capsulate themselves and spin reluctantly out of control to where we're not sure what is the truth and what is a lie.

This is exactly what the enemy wants us to do. He is the father of lies and wants us to believe his lies. When that happens, we must search for the truth. Dig deep into the well of life—the Word of God. Read, study, and talk about it with others. Give it your full attention because unlike a tornado, its calming, restful, and is the greatest method of understanding the Lord's ways. The book may not have all the answers you're looking for, but it has the answer above all—Jesus. It'll be your comfort pillow. A family Bible on a shelf gathers dust, but an opened Bible that's read brings life and fills our minds with understanding.

> My child, listen to what I say, and treasure my commands. Tune your ears to wisdom, and concentrate on understanding. Cry out for insight, and ask for understanding. Search for them as you would for silver; seek them like hidden treasure. Then you will understand what it means to fear the LORD, and you will gain knowledge of God. For the Lord grants wisdom! From his mouth come knowledge and understanding. He grants a treasure of common sense to the honest. He is a shield to those who walk with integrity. He guards the paths of the just and protects those who are faithful to him. Then you will understand what is right, just, and fair, and you will find the right way to go. For wisdom will enter your heart, and knowledge will fill you with joy. Wise choices will watch over you. Understanding will keep you safe. (Proverbs 2:1–11 NLT)

Verse 11 is so powerful and worthy of repeating: "Understanding will keep you safe." At first impression we wonder how will understanding keep us safe? If we have understanding, we know that we can't always be spontaneous and reckless. Sometimes we must think matters through and put together a plan to make it work. I certainly can't mop my tile floor before I sweep it. Otherwise, the mop is just flinging crumbs everywhere. Or how can I do laundry unless I think ahead and separate the clothes first? If I mix the new blue jeans with white clothes and bleach, there will obviously be a disaster.

Now, if I decide I want to go riding in the desert all day when it's ninety degrees outside, I can't just jump on the ATV and go for a ride. I need to put together a plan. I should most importantly pack water and sunscreen, and some lunch or snacks, and let someone know where I'm going. Otherwise I may get stranded, sunburned, and dehydrated, not a good combination by any means.

Understanding is so much more than that moment of an overhead lightbulb when we say, "Oh yeah, that's it." The Lord's understanding comes by searching as if we're hunting for lost treasure. Diligent. Persistent. Seeking. Tirelessly. It will never get old because we'll find gems of understanding every time.

Paul wrote in Colossians 2:2–3 (NIV),

> My goal is that they may be encouraged in heart and united in love, so that they may have the full riches of complete understanding, in order that they may know the mystery of God, namely, Christ, in whom are hidden all the treasures of wisdom and knowledge.

The Lord can take the most tragic story and make it into a victorious banner. Satan meant to destroy Sarah and, in turn, destroy me. But God has given me a new morning, a new mercy, a new hope for each tomorrow. I pray the promise of tomorrow will fill your today with cups of hope in abundance.

That's my desire for you as well, friend, that you spend planned time in your everyday life in the Word, and I promise you that you'll find thousands of treasures that will help you to know the ways of Him who desires you to come closer. And look deeper, no matter if you're just starting your life or nearing your finish. I'm so thankful that I don't have to trudge through the jungles of South America, or climb the snowy peaks of the Alps, or dig through hot sand in the summer heat of the Sahara Desert to find treasure to feel enriched. The Bible is an abundance of rich understanding and unconditional love that God wishes to lavish on us. A treasure of diamonds isn't a girl's best friend. The Word of God is.

> I have hidden your word in my heart that I might not sin against you. (Psalm 119:11 NLT)

Prayer of Trust

Savior of my heart, it's good to know that You hold me in the palm of Your hand and that You know everything. As much as I want to, I don't need to know everything. In the matters that I need wisdom, I pray that You will provide it to me. I pray that You'll help me to understand when it's Your will for me to understand. Even in those times in my life when it doesn't make sense to me, I will still trust in You. In the name of my trusting friend, Jesus. Amen.

CHAPTER 13

The Song

November 1, 1999

So we sing hallelujah, Christ has risen
And because He lives we know that she lives too.
—*Christian Joseph*

THE DAY WE RECEIVED A PHONE CALL FROM CHRIS BECAME a good day. Chris is a local musician and a good friend of our family for many years. Chris brought good news and with it came vision and hope.

"Hey, Ray. It's Chris."

"Chris, how are you doing?" Ray asked.

"Hey, man, I just wanted to call and tell you how sorry I am to hear about Sarah."

"Thank you. It's good to hear from you, Chris."

"I just can't believe it. Sarah was such a nice kid with a big smile that lit up a room. I am just in shock, man."

"Yeah, I know. We can't believe it either," Ray responded.

"I just saw Sarah like two weeks ago at my concert. I remember seeing her there, and she came up to talk to me after the concert was over. I just can't believe that she's gone."

Chris writes songs and performs them in our area. He also creates music videos and is well-known within our community.

"I'm not sure if this is the right time for this, but I have something to share with you and Sherri that I hope in some small way might help you. I just want to help," Chris said almost apologetically.

"Sure, Chris, let me put the phone on speakerphone so Sherri and I can both hear." Ray put the phone on speakerphone.

"Hey, Sherri. I wrote a song. I didn't set out to write a song. I just felt strongly compelled or drawn to write down my thoughts on the loss of Sarah. I thought maybe it would go into a journal or a poem, not necessarily to share, but maybe just for myself to make sense of this tremendous loss. I went into a room with my guitar, my Bible, a notebook, and a pencil. In my Bible I looked up verses on death, and the words started flowing out of me onto the paper. Then I started adding music to it, and it came so fast. Within three days I had written a song. What you need to understand, you guys, is that it usually takes me three or more months to write a song. This was finished in three days. It's crazy."

"It's a sad song but a hopeful song. The message of the song is that this is not the end. Death is not the end. God promises the hope of heaven, and I wanted to include that as the message. The bridge of the song appears to be the most meaningful, telling the story how Christ is risen, and that because Christ is risen, we know that Sarah lives too."

"Once I finished writing the song, I never intended to exploit it. I wanted it to be a gift to the both of you for encouragement and to bring hope. I don't want you to feel obligated to listen to it or maybe you don't even feel like you can listen to it, I don't know."

We gladly accepted the offer. In fact, we were very anxious to hear the song.

"I am in the middle of wrapping up the editing of my newest CD, and I want to add this song to the CD. But first, I want you to hear the song and tell me how you feel about it, and then possibly get your permission to include it on the CD."

Of course, Ray and I together emphatically said, "Yes, definitely."

Chris went on to tell us that he would mail us a copy of the demo cassette tape for us to listen to first. He described the song as simple, very general. He told us that he didn't have a title for the song yet, so he just called it "For Sarah."

A few days later, Ray walked into our house with the day's mail, told me the tape had come, and asked if I was ready to listen to it. As I slid the cassette tape into the tape player, my hand shook. I was so anxious to hear it. I had no idea what it would be like, other than it was about hope. As the music played, I was amazed, humbled, and touched. The song was all about our Sarah Renee, something I didn't expect at all, and the hope of heaven that came from her death.

When he sang, "So we sing hallelujah, Christ has risen, and because He lives we know that she lives too," I felt a presence, and in that presence, I felt promise. I cried happy tears that day. It was better than I ever imagined. I listened to it again and again.

Chris told us days later that the recording of the song happened quickly. He managed to get a friend to play guitar in the studio and then added some guitar himself. Chris reflected on how fast it came together.

Chris was about to release his newest album days before but felt impressed upon that he needed to delay the release date and include Sarah's song on the CD. He wasn't sure if that was possible, but he was going to try. After days of many struggles and rivers he had to cross to get the song on the CD, the CD was released a few weeks later. The song was simply entitled "For Sarah."[4]

Ray and I decided to invite Chris to play music for a get-together with Sarah's friends that we planned as part of our homecoming in mid-November. The song would be perfect.

Once the burial was over and everyone went on their way back to their daily lives, we were lonely. We missed family and friends being so close for those first couple of weeks. We also missed Sarah's friends whom we had connected with. Ray and I felt a special connection with her friends, many we didn't even know. Seeing them and hugging them was an unexplainable closeness that somehow made us feel closer to our daughter.

I prepared finger foods including Sarah's favorite candy treat, peanut butter cups. Several of Sarah's friends came. We had my brother come to take photographs for memories and for photos of the friends

---

4 "For Sarah," 2000, Christian Joseph (a.k.a. Chris Commisso) (ASCAP) used by permission, "For Sarah" now available on most streaming platforms; and video entitled "Sarah Renee Cullison" by Ray Cullison on https://www.youtube.com/watch?v=z2jhVQQkZZo.

together as a keepsake for them. Chris agreed to come and entertain with his music. For the first time, he sang "For Sarah" to her friends. Hearts were touched and tears flowed, but most importantly the hope that Sarah was now in Jesus's arms was shared. There was some laughter and a few smiles. Not many of her friends ate. They sat in groups and chatted together and then mingled with others. A couple of her classmates wandered into Sarah's and Namantha's bedroom, just to be closer to her memory, I imagine.

Ray found one of Sarah's friends sitting on her bed alone, and she was crying. He asked her what was wrong, and she told him that Sarah was the only person who said she was beautiful on the days she felt ugly. And now that Sarah was gone, she had no one to encourage her and make her feel pretty and loved. A bittersweet moment. We never knew that about Sarah. We never knew that although she was feeling unloved and ugly, she was telling someone else that they were beautiful and loved.

Has anyone ever told you that you're beautiful? Has anyone ever said to you that you're enough? There have been times in my life where I felt worthless and at the very least, ugly. Sometimes the lies came gradually and sometimes quickly. And when they did, I sank into what felt like a deep ocean of loneliness. The more I thought of myself as unbeautiful, the more I believed it.

My spirit felt heavier and heavier as though I was swimming in the ocean miles from shore. With each wave of self-doubt and unbelief, I drifted away from the safety of shore, and it felt like someone was pulling me under, deeper and deeper. I tried flailing my arms, desperately groping to reach the surface of the water. I gasped for air but only choked on the swirling current that pulled me under further. I thought I was alone with no one in sight. No one was there to reassure me that I was pretty, that I was enough. I thought no one was there to give me hope. Then in a moment of faith, I reached out, whispering a desperate prayer. As if a rescue boat appeared out of nowhere and threw a rope to me in the water, I frantically reached for the line that pulled me to safety. I just needed to stretch out my arm and grasp ahold of the lifeline that pulled me in closer. I then felt relief. I felt safe. I no longer felt alone.

> The Lord is good, a strong refuge when trouble comes. He is close to those who trust in Him. (Nahum 1:7 NLT)

Sometimes we need to remember that God is a reach away. Yes, God is always with us. But He wants us to *require* Him. He wants us to make the effort and reach out for His lifeline. He is able to rescue you from any desperate situation you may be in. The circumstances of life may be overwhelming you, and you're drowning in your world. But the Rescuer never fails. He revived me when I felt like I could no longer keep my head above water. He rescued me when I was unconscious in my drowning. I began to panic when I realized that I couldn't save myself and my spirit fainted.

Perhaps you're at the end of the rescue rope and you feel you don't have the strength left to hold on. Maybe you're holding onto the rope and simply want to let go. Please don't let go. Give it one more tug. Then another. Reach out to a lifeline and tell someone you're drowning. Tell a friend, a pastor, or counselor, a crisis hotline. Tell God.

> He reached down from heaven and rescued me; he drew me out of deep waters. He led me to a place of safety; he rescued me because he delights in me. (Psalm 18:16, 19 NLT)

Prayer of Rescue

Father God, I thank You that You're always there to reach up to and pull me out of the restraint that holds on so tight sometimes. I'm thankful that Your hand is only a reach away. Sometimes I don't have to reach up. You simply save me. And sometimes I have to reach up to You, to *want* You to save me. But You're always there, always ready when I'm ready. In the name of my Rescuer, Jesus. Amen.

CHAPTER 14

The Trip

Summer, 2000

This is what the Lord says: "In the time of my favor I will answer you, and in the day of salvation I will help you; I will keep you and will make you to be a covenant for the people, to restore the land and to reassign its desolate inheritances, to say to the captives, 'Come out,' and to those in darkness, 'Be free!'"
Isaiah 49:8–9 (NIV)

WHILE IT SEEMS OUR LOSSES AND HEARTBREAKS ARE FULL of only pain and sorrow, let me assure you that God can use the most devastating life experience to help others. Ray and I both have shared Sarah's story many times, and several people have told us that they were touched by her story. Others told us how they have struggled with the loss of family members to suicide and others who were suicidal.

Later the next year, while on staff as worship leader/music director at our church, our church secretary had received a brochure from Jay Lowder of Harvest Ministries, an evangelist located in Texas. Our pastor called Jay's office to inquire about his availability to teach for a revival. Our church was small, around three hundred members, and our community was small, approximately twenty thousand people. Jay relayed to the pastor that normally the brochures are mailed to much larger churches in bigger cities. He couldn't explain how the brochure got to our little church in Kingman, Arizona; however, he indicated that there must be a reason he needed to come to preach for this revival.

Jay generally speaks to teens at schools about the dangers of alcohol, drugs, and suicide. During the revival, we asked if Jay could go to lunch with us before he left to go home.

Jay wanted to hear Sarah's story, so we told him everything. Among many people talking, dishes clanging, doors opening and closing, and waitress interruptions, we told Jay the circumstances before, during, and after Sarah's death. He listened with attentive ears, devout eyes, and respectful and responsive words. Jay's own personal testimony includes his near attempt at suicide when he was college age.

"I'd like to ask you both a question. When I speak and minister, whether it be crowds at churches or to kids and teens at school assemblies, would you consider allowing me to share your daughter's story? I believe it would have a great impact of bringing people, especially teens, to know Christ."

"Of course," Ray and I both said simultaneously.

That conversation started a special friendship. We're convinced the one purpose Jay was meant to come to the revival was for us to meet and for Jay to share Sarah's story. Jay kept in contact with us every few months to keep us aware of when he shared Sarah's story. Literally thousands have heard her story and either gained hope where there was none, rededicated their lives with a new beginning, or accepted Jesus in their hearts. We rejoice because of this, despite having lost a precious life in our family. Jesus died on the cross for all our sins including Sarah's, but there was also another redemption for our daughter's life. Thousands of people are now saved and going to heaven because of Sarah's story.

In March of 2012, Ray was speaking to one of Jay's staff members on the phone and Ray had been struggling. Our daughter Namantha had asked him to post on social media the video he had made that included the song, "For Sarah." This was a video compilation of various videos that I had taken of Sarah or videos she had taken of herself. (View the song lyrics "For Sarah" in the back of the book.)

While the staff member asked Ray to pray for the upcoming revival Jay would be teaching, Ray asked the staff member for prayer about his current struggle. The staff member called Ray back on Monday to see how he was doing and to give a report from the revival.

"I'm not really sure why or even if it's possible, since arrangements have already been made, but I think you need to go to Northern Ireland with us in June." He shared with Ray how Jay and several family members and himself would be traveling to Northern Ireland where Jay would speak at a city-wide event entitled Mission Hope.

Ray shared this with me, and we discussed whether we could even afford to go.

"Ireland? Really?" I asked, amazed. "We could probably afford for you to go, but not both of us."

Ray waited for confirmation, and even though God gave him a couple of indications that this was His will, Ray continued to search for an answer.

Ray knew that the suicide rate in Northern Ireland was extremely high—one every thirty-six hours. He searched the internet just to see what we were getting ourselves into and what to expect. He typed, "Lurgan, Northern Ireland, teen suicides." The very first search engine that popped up was titled, "Hi, I'm Sarah, I'm fourteen, and I want to commit suicide."

Ray leaned back in his chair, threw open his arms, and said, "Okay, God, you win." The Lord couldn't have shouted His will much louder than that. And if that wasn't enough challenge to God, Ray prayed, "God, if you want me to go, you're going to have to provide a way financially."

For the next few short weeks, Ray and I worked together traveling and speaking to various churches in our area where we had served in the past, sharing this mission opportunity and asking if they would help us financially to go. Ray had determined that we collected enough money to cover the trip of Mission Hope. We wanted to be good stewards of the money we had collected so we stopped seeking financial aid. Within two weeks we had collected enough from so many generous people for both of us to make the trip.

Within a few days, Ray realized he had made a mistake on the financial estimate for the trip. We were flying into Dublin, and the money exchange for that country, Ireland, was the euro. But the plans involved us driving immediately into Northern Ireland for the remainder of the trip before we drove back to Dublin. The money exchange for Northern Ireland was the British pound. The problem we faced was an error of five hundred dollars we didn't have. The days on the calendar were counting down to leave for the trip, and it appeared that we needed to call on more churches. We were disappointed that we needed to ask for more financial help.

The next day Ray received a phone call from our former church secretary stating more money had come in from people giving, and she asked him to pick up the check. She indicated it wasn't much, but it was something to help. Ray stopped by the church office the next morning and then called me on the phone.

"Sherri, I went by the church and picked up the check," Ray said, his voice breaking. There was a long pause.

"The check is for five hundred and seventy-five dollars."

We were lost in bewilderment of the wonder of God. We knew this was the direct work of His hand. He filled a need and He filled our hearts. We were so humbled and so thankful.

In less than two months later, we were on a plane to Ireland. The beauty of the Irish homeland was outstanding, and the wonderful pastors and wives involved in the orchestration of Mission Hope were all so very kind. With the Northern Ireland Conflict between the Irish Republican Army and the Protestant Loyalists re-emerging in the late 1960s, the protestants and the Catholics were divided. They lived in separate buildings, they went to separate schools, separate churches, and murals all over the cities evidenced their hate for one another, even following the Good Friday peace treaty of April 10, 1998.[5]

A group of pastors, ministers, and priests coordinated Mission Hope, a week-long schedule where everyone from every church was invited to attend and listen to Jay's messages. They called on the people to unite for this event for the Lord, and, in fact, many expected a small turnout. The first night over two thousand people showed up at Shankill

---

5 Northern Ireland Conflict, *Good Friday Agreement*, June 6, 2008, www.brittanica.com

Parish Church of Christ the Redeemer, a church building built in 1725 in the center of the town Lurgan.[6] God chose a church in the center of the city to unite all denominations. It was an event never before attempted. Some feared violence, even retaliation, but God brought peace.

Jay brought messages each night anointed with eloquence and strong conviction. Each night many people came forward to give their hearts to Jesus or rededicate their lives, and some came forward for prayer needs. It was amazing to be in a room filled with hundreds of people where God's Spirit engulfed each night.

Ray and I were asked to share Sarah's story on Saturday night, the last night of Mission Hope. We were honored, but honestly, it was hard—emotionally hard. I was anxious to bring hope to others amid so much suffering, yet I had to expose my life in front of thousands I did not know. My conviction to help others far outweighed my shame and fear of others' opinion. So many people attending had lost family members and close friends to suicide, and that was the purpose for our being there. To help. To encourage. To let God use us to save lives and spare the pain, the sorrow, and the hopelessness for others. There was no doubt in my mind that this was God's will for us.

After we spoke that night, a few people approached us and shared how they were encouraged by us sharing our testimony, and they thanked us.

I noticed a man in his forties, holding a woman by her arm and pushing her gently up to me. The expression on his face was of necessity. The woman looked peaceful with a gentle smile on her face. She was probably in her forties, with short dark hair. She was a beautiful woman yet looked worn with the world's troubles on her face.

She approached me and said, "Thank you so much for sharing your story about your daughter. She was beautiful. I have struggled with depression all my life and have attempted suicide several times. I know God loves me, but I fight this oppressive disease every day. I was invited to this event but wrestled with the thought of coming all day."

---

6 S. J. Malcolm, *Shankill* Parish Church, www.lurganancestry.com.

Amid loud chatter and a crowd lingering in the lobby of this ancient building, we stood there listening intently.

"You saved my life tonight," she said with inclination. I tried to discount myself any credit, but she insisted.

"You sharing your story tonight saved my life." She paused. "What you don't understand is that tonight I was going to kill myself."

We were astounded at her confession. We immediately encouraged her to cling to her faith in God, to hope for the future He had planned, thanked her for sharing something so private and so difficult, and referred her to someone to counsel her.

Look what the Lord did. I was amazed, astonished. I felt a heavy burden for her struggle, yet a peace in knowing we did the right thing by traveling thousands of miles to be there at that very moment sharing our hurt and sorrow, just so this woman would live another day.

As people came to thank us, I watched a man slowly move his way closer to us, obviously wrestling with wanting to talk to us but also appearing very hesitant. Finally, he reached us and shared how he worked as a police officer for many years. He told us how he had come upon many calls where a suicide victim had been found. He told us how hard it was for him to see these scenes over and over. It was a traumatic experience every time.

As he spoke his voice quivered. He nervously fidgeted with the hat in his hand as he spilled his heart to us. His eyes revealed pain and pleas for help. He didn't know how to cope with it.

I told him how sorry I was that he had to experience this and thanked him for coming to talk with us. What a huge step of courage it was for him to step forward to share his deepest, darkest pain. I suggested that he should find counsel, perhaps even his own pastor, and that he should continue to seek the Lord for consolation and wisdom.

Many, many lives were saved in Northern Ireland that week, and we were there to witness this miracle of unity and love. This trip brought hope to so many, even me.

In conclusion, unfortunately our human minds try to convince us that nothing good could ever come from such a horrific tragedy of losing my youngest child to suicide, but look, friend. Look what the Lord has done. So many words, so many hugs, so many blessings, so many lives changed because of one loss.

What is missing in your life? Is it hope? Is it God? Life may look bleak in your eyes and you may be drowning in a sea of despair, but the good news I have for you is that God is there for you. He loves you. He wants to bless you and wants to work your devastating circumstance around for good. Simply ask Him into your life and for help in your circumstance.

How will you overcome depression, anxiety, and loss? One day at a time. Seek Him. Talk to Him and read His Word, His love letter to you. Worship Him for who He is, your Rescuer.

> And we know that in all things God works for the good of those who love Him, who have been called according to his purpose. (Romans 8:28 NIV)

As I mentioned in chapter one, I lost Sarah's stone from my mother's ring before I lost her. Then the stone was replaced and the restoration began. Again in 2019, before I wrote this book, I was putting on my jewelry and looked down at my hand at my mother's ring. Sarah's ruby stone was gone from the ring *again*. What? How could that be? How could the stone that was replaced also fall out? I tried to resist panic when my hands started to shake and tears welled up in my eyes. My eyes darted frantically across the tile throughout our home. I rubbed my hands through the carpet near my jewelry box. Nothing. My shoulders dropped in disappointment. Once again, I was forced to put the ring away until I could replace the stone.

The discouragement and loss I felt when I realized the stone in my ring was gone that spring day years later had somehow become an epiphany. What had been gifted to me was lost, then restored, and now lost again.

Perhaps my writing journey about Sarah has been the second loss I've had to experience and compress my heart all over again. But this time it's different. I know that restoration is coming.

I know deep down in the searches of my heart that there was a purpose in this loss of her stone, just as I know there is a purpose in the loss of Sarah, and maybe the purpose is you.

As I wrote this story of my beloved Sarah, I was reminded of my hurts, my shame, my heartache, and my regrets, and to an extent I experienced Sarah's loss all over again. But I know that I'll restore the ruby stone to my mother's ring one day. And just like the stone in my ring, God will continue to restore the emptiness of her loss. The hope in my heart increases knowing that one day He'll restore me completely in heaven when I run into His arms and into the arms of my little girl.

Prayer of Restoration

Father, You are the Guiding Light over the darkness of the tumultuous seas of my life. I acknowledge that You are holy, yet approachable, and that You have the ability to restore what's been lost in my life. Humbly, I bring my troubles, big and small, before You and ask You to help me find Your lifeline. Rescue me and restore me as you fill me with the promise of hope for tomorrow. In the name of Jesus, the One who restores me. Amen.

We might see you next week, Sarah, we're not sure.
We might see you next month, Sarah, we're not sure.
We might see you next year, Sarah, we're not sure.
We only know you'll be there waiting for us.
—Christian Joseph

Sarah's Poem

Thank You, God
by Sarah Renee Cullison
July 7, 1999

The day you saved me was the day I cared.
I'll always worship you, I'm always there.

Since you came in my life, you changed me all around.
You picked me up when I was down.

You made me see what I didn't know before.
I'm glad I let you come through my door.

The door that opened my heart; that was to love you.
Now I know things I never knew.

How great it is to have you in my life, and you will not leave
'Cause my dream you brought it true, God. I love You.

Together forever, that's how we'll always be.
No longer will I see the sadness.

Since You brought my life happiness,
Now You're a part of me.

Now, for everyone can see
I'm a believer in You when you told me—

Told me everything I didn't know.
I'm glad you set me free.

"For Sarah"

Sarah Renee
A wounded soul who only shared her smile but not her pain
Just a flower in bloom
That the rivers of destruction washed away too soon
And though we long to see her smiling face
We know that she is safe in Jesus's arms.
So, we won't cry for Sarah
Though we miss our Sarah
No sad goodbyes for Sarah
No, we won't cry for Sarah
Because we'll be home to see her soon.

Sarah Renee
We know that we will hold her in our arms again someday
So, we'll try to move on
And never live our lives as though all hope is gone.
Though heaven didn't need another angel
We know it's probably brighter cuz she's there.
So, we won't cry for Sarah
Though we miss our Sarah
No sad goodbyes for Sarah
No, we won't cry for Sarah
Cuz we'll be home to see her soon.

(Bridge)
Oh, death where is your sting
Oh grave, where is your victory
Cuz we know that Sarah's hope lies in the empty tomb of the man from Galilee.
So, we sing hallelujah
Christ has risen
And because He lives, we know that she lives too.

So, we won't cry for Sarah
Though we miss our Sarah
No sad goodbyes for Sarah
We won't cry for Sarah
Cuz we'll be home to see her soon.

We might see you next week, Sarah, we're not sure.
We might see you next month, Sarah, we're not sure.
We might see you next year, Sarah, we're not sure.
We only know you'll be there waiting for us.

Resources

Website: www.sherrijcullison.com

To schedule Sherri for a speaking engagement or other purpose, you may email her at heart4jc78@gmail.com or sherri@sherrijcullison.com.

Facebook: Sherri J. Cullison, Author
Instagram: sherrijcullison
Twitter: Sherri J Cullison

Jay Lowder, Harvest Ministries: www.jaylowder.com
Facebook & Twitter: Jay Lowder
Instagram: jay_lowder

Dawn Wilson: www.upgradewithdawn.com

American Foundation for Suicide Prevention: www.afsp.org
If you need help, call 1–800–273–8255 or text TALK to 741741

ORDER INFORMATION

REDEMPTION
PRESS

To order additional copies of this book, please visit
www.redemption-press.com.
Also available on Amazon.com and BarnesandNoble.com
or by calling toll-free 1-844-2REDEEM.

CPSIA information can be obtained
at www.ICGtesting.com
Printed in the USA
BVHW060008111121
621201BV00008B/487